"If you were to anticipate how strong a company's culture needs to be to transform and thrive in the future, Joey Havens paints a beautiful horizon in his book, *Leading with Significance*. He not only takes us on a journey to see and feel the power of magnetic energy in the workplace; you will also find anticipatory nuggets to navigate our own unique journey. Learn how a people-first mindset creates a strong sense of belonging where team members connect their purpose, values, and dreams and give discretionary efforts for innovation and high performance. Being anticipatory is threaded throughout this journey to build a powerful magnetic culture. Read this book today!"

—DANIEL BURRUS, author of seven best-selling books, including the *New York Times* and *Wall Street Journal* bestsellers *Flash Foresight* and *The Anticipatory Organization*

"Joey Havens has written one of, if not *the*, most compelling and in-depth books on culture and its power on organizational success today. The power of this book is not only the message, but that it is written from personal experience and showcases the long journey Joey took with his team to transform who they are as leaders and how they used their commitment and dedication to culture to transform their organization and their industry. Chock-full of stories, strategies, and ideas, this innovative read will not only keep you engaged, it will give you the motivation and ideas you need to implement this same type of transformation in your own business. Get this book. I promise you it will be one of the best investments you have made in a long time."

—MERIDITH ELLIOTT POWELL, top 15 business growth strategist, top 50 business speaker, and author of best-selling *THRIVE: Strategies to Turn Uncertainty to Competitive Advantage*

"This book is needed more than ever as employers and employees search for meaning and purpose at work. Joey Havens challenges us to all beBetter by showing us the playbook to create winning cultures that people want to work for, in a world where engaged employers are at all-time lows. Through his journey as managing partner in one of the top CPA firms, he shows the way to build a magnetic firm that attracts, retains, and develops people in a never-ending cause to constantly beBetter. We need this book and message more than ever."

—TOM HOOD, CPA, CGMA, executive vice president of business growth and engagement at AICPA-CIMA

"As I've traveled the world with John Maxwell over the past two decades, I've noticed a common trend: many people struggle with finding purpose and meaning in the workplace. That's why I'm so thankful for this book, *Leading with Significance*! Finding purpose begins with finding significance, and finding significance begins with valuing people. The culture of your organization will become magnetic and powerful as people become committed to serve each other and pursue a common purpose together. In this book, Joey has laid out a flexible road map that will help you chart your own journey of creating a culture that truly values people. I am better because of this book, and I'm confident you will be too!"

—MARK COLE, owner/CEO, Maxwell Leadership

LEADING

with

SIGNIFICANCE

How to Create a Magnetic,
People-First Culture

JOEY HAVENS

GREENLEAF
BOOK GROUP PRESS

Published by Greenleaf Book Group Press
Austin, Texas
www.gbgpress.com

Distributed by Greenleaf Book Group

For ordering information or special discounts for bulk purchases,
please contact Greenleaf Book Group at PO Box 91869, Austin, TX
78709, 512.891.6100.

With grateful acknowledgment, the beBetter logo is used with
permission of HORNE LLC and content from the blog post "Three
Strategies to Create Full Team Engagement" is used with permission of
Meridith Elliott Powell © 2022.

Design and composition by Greenleaf Book Group
Cover design by Greenleaf Book Group

Publisher's Cataloging-in-Publication data is available.

Print ISBN: 979-8-88645-048-4

eBook ISBN: 979-8-88645-049-1

To offset the number of trees consumed in the printing of our books,
Greenleaf donates a portion of the proceeds from each printing to
the Arbor Day Foundation. Greenleaf Book Group has replaced over
50,000 trees since 2007.

Printed in the United States of America on acid-free paper

23 24 25 26 27 28 29. 30   10 9 8 7 6 5 4 3 2 1

First Edition

To Cathy, my wife, who wears the crown of "CeCe" in our family. Thanks for all your love, support, and sacrifices. Thanks for helping me beBetter. You are an amazing blessing to me.

To Mom and Pop Joe, you have loved me despite my flaws. You taught me Christian values, but better yet, you live them daily. Forever grateful for teaching me the love of God.

And to my partners and team members at HORNE, words can't express my joy, gratitude, and appreciation for taking me along on such an incredible journey of honoring God, service above self, and caring for others.

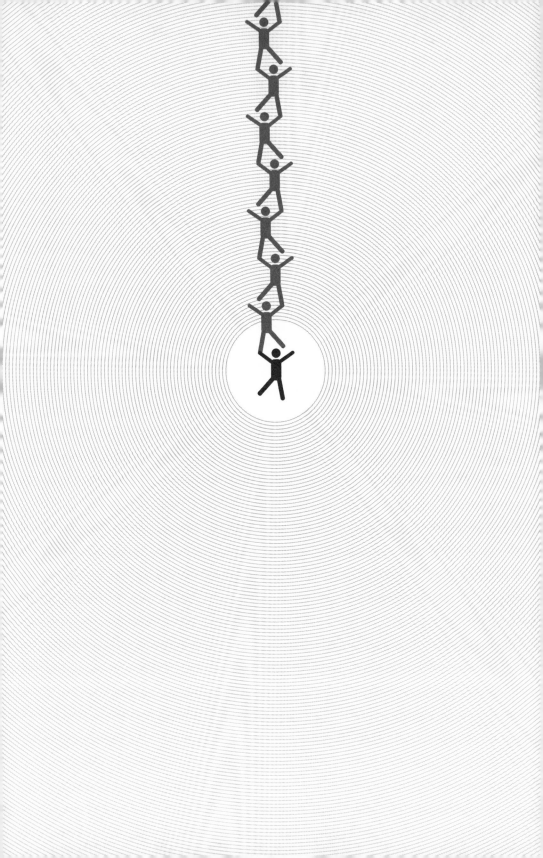

Contents

INTRODUCTION

What's Possible

IS IT POSSIBLE TO CREATE and grow a magnetic culture in the middle of the Great Resignation, in the wake of the pandemic, in the turbulence of technology transformation impacting every organization?

ABSOLUTELY!

Is it possible to generate magnetic energy that actually creates a competitive advantage and attracts talent?

ABSOLUTELY!

So if it's possible, why are so many organizations struggling as more people demonstrate their dissatisfaction with today's workplace culture by disengaging or walking away? We are experiencing a culture clash and disconnection like never before. Sadly, too many leaders and team members either quit when the going gets hard or they simply don't really believe they can make a difference, don't believe they can create a magnetic culture that people want to be part of.

Over the year or so as this book was coming together, a phenomenon labeled the Great Resignation or the Great Reevaluation was boiling over throughout the United States. Department of Labor statistics[1] show that we have just experienced over 4 million people quitting their current jobs 11 months in a row through April 2022. We are faced with accelerating turnover and a desperate searching for top-tier talent. Burnout is rampant, even with our most loyal team members. Surveys[2] indicate that over 40 percent of team members today are considering a move from their present company. Let that sink in a minute; it's a pretty scary thought.

Although the ramifications of the COVID-19 pandemic have been a frequently cited cause for the mass exodus, the workforce has responded with feedback pointing directly at a call for better culture. In extreme circumstances, a toxic work culture is driving the turnover, but the biggest culprit is what we generously call *good culture*. These "good" culture workplaces leave people feeling interchangeable, with little connection, low levels of trust, energy, and appreciation, and sensing a lack of a voice, meaning, purpose, and belonging.

Cultures that cling to their status quo "good" culture react to each crisis rather than being intentional about proactively caring for people. According to McKinsey & Company's blog, "More than half of employees who left their job in the past six months did not feel valued by their organization (54 percent) or manager (52 percent), or they lacked a sense of belonging (51 percent). Additionally, 46 percent cited the desire to work with people who trust and care for each other as another reason to quit."[3]

---

1   US Bureau of Labor Statistics, "Table 4: Quits Levels and Rates by Industry and Region, Seasonally Adjusted," Economic News Release, July 6, 2022, https://www.bls.gov/news.release/jolts.t04.htm.

2   Hinge Marketing, *Culture Clash: The Employee Experience Problem and How to Fix It*, Hinge Research Institute (2022); Greg Iarurci, "'The War for Talent' Continues. 40% of Recent Job Switchers Are Again Looking for a New Position, Survey Finds," CNBC "Life Changes," April 11, 2022, https://www.cnbc.com/2022/04/11/40percent-of-job-switchers-already-looking-for-new-positions-survey-finds.html; Aaron De Smet, Bonnie Dowling, Marino Mugayar-Baldocchi, and Bill Schaninger, "'Great Attrition' or 'Great Attraction'? The Choice Is Yours," *McKinsey Quarterly*, September 8, 2021, https://www.mckinsey.com/business-functions/people-and-organizational-performance/our-insights/great-attrition-or-great-attraction-the-choice-is-yours.

3   Aaron De Smet, Bonnie Dowling, Marino Mugayar-Baldocchi, and Joe Spratt, "It's Not about the Office, It's about Belonging," McKinsey.com (blog), January 13, 2022, https://www.mckinsey.com/business-functions/people-and-organizational-performance/our-insights/the-organization-blog/its-not-about-the-office-its-about-belonging.

This big exodus of talent and brewing unrest beneath the surface indicate that people are reevaluating what they want from work and who they want to work for and with. They are searching for a sense of belonging, a community, a tribe where they can help build a better culture and foster people-first intentionality.

Arianna Huffington has recast the Great Resignation as the Great Reevaluation. She contends that people are abandoning not so much their individual jobs but an entire culture of burnout and a misguided interpretation of success.[4] People are voting with their feet when they say they want to live and work in a completely different manner.

MISSING THE MARK

Companies are rapidly responding with more compensation, more benefits, and more people initiatives, but they are missing the mark. They are aiming too low while clinging to their status quo "good" culture. Free lunches, casual dress, pets welcome, Friday off, more flexibility—these and more are all in the headlines. These are all fads that do not address the real meaning and purpose of work or the heart of today's growing dissatisfaction. They are Band-Aids that can increase mediocrity, complacency, and entitlement when core issues of culture are ignored. This miss is resulting in a wave of regret where people leave one company for another, only to find the new organization's culture is just as bad—or worse. "By not understanding what their employees are running from," says McKinsey & Company, "and what they might gravitate to, company leaders are putting their very businesses at risk."[5]

When a company might be moving in the right direction with some

---

4   Arianna Huffington, "People Aren't Just Quitting Their Jobs. They're Redefining Success: Why the Great Resignation Is about More than Burnout," *Inc.*, June 30, 2021, https://www.inc.com/arianna-huffington/people-arent-just-quitting-their-jobs-theyre-redefining-success.html.

5   De Smet et al., "'Great Attrition' or 'Great Attraction'? The Choice Is Yours."

initiatives, too often, the culture itself is not strong enough to support the initiative. This is why so many of our diversity-and-inclusion initiatives are failing to get the results we all want and expect. These "good" cultures are not inclusive enough, not strong enough, to support significant change. You begin to see silos within companies rather than inclusion and high performance. We forget that inclusion and high performance are choices that individuals must make every day to be successful. "Good" culture is not good enough.

INTENTIONALITY, COURAGE, BELONGING

The core message of this book could not possibly be more relevant to our current situation. The pulse of this book is how you can build and experience a magnetic workplace. It's a journey that dives into the core issues of creating a magnetic culture and pulls back the curtains to reveal the challenges and human emotions that become stumbling blocks for so many. Whether you are a C-suite leader, middle management, a consultant, or a front-line team member in your organization, you can use the wisdom, lessons learned, and experiences from this book to build a better culture. Everyone in your organization can learn from this book. You can help grow a strong sense of belonging and can be intentionally significant in people's lives. It is possible to turn the tide on the Great Resignation and become a magnet for talent searching for purpose and belonging.

To that end, I'll use our experiences to help you understand the journey we continue to travel at HORNE LLP, a professional services firm with a CPA cornerstone. But this is by no means a book about HORNE. Rather, it's a story about intentionally building and pursuing a culture of greatness and high performance. It's about building a magnetic culture that attracts talent and, in turn, the magnetic energy that creates a *wow!* experience for clients. It's also a story of emotion and the highs and lows of the journey. Is the painful process to build something special worth it?

Needless to say, the stories I share won't make building a magnetic culture easy. There is nothing easy about challenging the status quo and doing the hard work of intentionally designing your culture. You will find lots of mistakes along our journey—mistakes that you can hopefully avoid. This journey is complicated and difficult, riddled with moments of anger, disappointment, fear, negativity, self-doubt, unworthiness, and, frankly, weariness.

It's my hope that HORNE's story serves as inspiration for your journey—a helpful, instructive example highlighting key insights for success and providing a peek under the tent of building a magnetic workplace. To that end, the story will also provide insights from our mistakes along the way. This book will not make your journey easier, but it will help you see that it is possible. Moreover, you'll come to understand that every bit of the struggle, every challenge you may encounter, is absolutely worth it.

Building a magnetic culture isn't just a matter of introducing certain initiatives and programs and watching what happens. There are powerful dynamics that not only drive such efforts but also ensure their acceptance. Complex, often uncomfortable human emotions and actions such as loving, caring, advocating, forgiving, and respecting need to be recognized for their roles in crafting a culture that's both genuine and enduring. This type of journey mandates multiple levels of transparency, including the courage to be absolutely open and honest about the emotions that accompany it and that, for many of us, are difficult to talk about.

As you will see in stories and anecdotes throughout the book, building the Wise Firm (the name we gave our culture) involved a great many emotional and even painful moments, but they were pivotal events even if they were later clearly mistakes and missteps. Moreover, they didn't just simply occur; they, in fact, *had* to happen, or our journey would have inevitably faltered.

As a matter of fact, the courage to be transparent was a challenge that even came up in the writing of this book. Often, it was a struggle to address—really address, not merely skirt over—the critical values that must serve as the guardrails for any great company or organization: caring, forgiveness, advocacy, and empathy, to cite just a few. In sharing the story, in the beginning, it seemed as though those discussions might come off as indulgent or focus too much on any one person or group. But it became clear that to advocate transparency, this book would have to be every bit as transparent. Lacking that, HORNE's journey toward the Wise Firm would seem unduly clinical, which was anything but the case. Looking back, countless team members and others put themselves out on emotional and professional limbs to help move our journey forward.

MAGNETIC THOUGHTS

Each chapter concludes with a bulleted feature titled "Magnetic Thoughts." Referring to the magnetic energy that is so central to this book is designed not only to reinforce significant points covered in that particular chapter but also to reconnect those points to those emotional dynamics that were so much a force in building our Wise Firm culture and generating our magnetic energy.

Phrased another way, they're ideas and observations that warrant particular attention. You will find stories, insights, and magnetic thoughts around these key concepts:

- Embracing the brutal reality of status quo "good" culture

- A compelling vision—people first

- A beBetter mindset

- Flexibility as unique for the individual and extending far beyond the workplace

- A sense of belonging defining inclusion that releases the power of diversity

- Demonstrated caring

- Sponsorship and advocacy

- Feedback, coaching, and full potential

- A committed leadership team

- Understanding the coincidences of God, faith, and culture

- Choosing significance first

Just like the key concepts above, as you reflect on these magnetic thoughts and insights, ask yourself the following questions:

- How does this story relate to our culture today?

- Are there opportunities in our organization to beBetter? To be magnetic?

- How are we promoting a sense of community, a tribe, building something together?

- How can we use the strengths of our present culture to accelerate our journey toward a magnetic culture?

- How does our leadership demonstrate people first? Do we recognize the good in people?

- Where does culture sit in our strategic plan?

- Do our leaders understand that people believe what they see and experience, not what we say? How really flexible are our flexibility policies?

- What percentage of our team members would rate their sense of belonging as strong?

- Do our team members trust each other and trust our leadership?

- How transparent have we been on people-first progress? On diversity and inclusion? On turnover?

- Do our team members all have access to sponsors? Coaches?

- Are we really reaching our full potential as team members?

- Do we promote learning fast, learning forward, and learning together?

- Are we "too nice" as an organization due to conflict avoidance?

- Are we moving fast enough?

- Do we tolerate or make excuses for toxic leaders?

- Does every voice count?

COINCIDENCES OF GOD, FAITH, AND CULTURE

Enjoy the unexpected coincidences in our journey as we found God, faith, and culture intersecting, connecting, and elevating us at every turn. It's certainly an opportunity to stop and reflect: Are there really any coincidences when it comes to God? I believe we are called to love one another. We can demonstrate that love in our workplace by caring and serving those we work with. A sense of belonging grows as we trust, believe, and recognize the good in people. People are searching for organizations that truly care and demonstrate a people-first mindset. They are seeking teams with strong character and leadership that is trustworthy. There's an innate longing to be part of something bigger than themselves. People want meaning and purpose in their work. They are looking for that magnetic energy!

You will see in our journey that we believe we can honor God by doing all of these things. God created us with this need to connect to others, and it's no surprise to me that, when you find a truly magnetic culture, God and faith are playing a big role. This is certainly true for our journey. At times during the book and at the end of each chapter, I've shared key Bible verses that I relied on during our journey. These verses helped grow my faith, provided me with inspiration, and helped me focus on people first. Maybe one of these biblical nuggets will help grow your faith or inspire you to seek a better understanding of God's role and power in building a magnetic culture.

It is my sincere hope that, as you read this book, you discover ideas, uncover wisdom, and develop insights that can help you beBetter and inspire you to lead your organization on a journey to building a magnetic culture.

1

Good Culture Is
Not Good Enough

AS HARD AS IT MAY be to believe, two pounds of rotting hamburger meat taught me an invaluable lesson about company culture.

Growing up in Mississippi, I managed to save up $300 by the time I was 15 years old. I knew just where I wanted that money to go. My daddy took me up to Memphis, and we found a 1965 Ford Falcon with a stick shift, priced at $300. Daddy said he would pay the insurance, so I bought the car, brought it home, and promptly painted it as part of my Future Farmers of America project.

I can't tell you how proud I was of that car. This 1965 Ford Falcon was my independence. I was ready and eager to do anything that needed to be done, so long as it involved that car—including hauling my younger brother Mike around and running errands for my mother.

Not long thereafter, I went shopping for a cookout with friends. I put a bunch of groceries in the trunk, took them out when I got to the cookout, and didn't give them another thought.

A week later, my car started having a very unpleasant odor, so I cleaned it top to bottom. The next week, the car was stinking like crazy, so I cleaned it inside and out again! Since I was riding in it every day, I began keeping the windows wide open, thinking the fresh air would help solve the problem. It did provide some temporary relief, but it didn't last.

Every time I picked somebody up, they'd immediately make a face and demand, "Dang, what's the smell in your car?" Instead of facing the reality that my car had a terrible stench, I justified, rationalized, and even denied it. I just kept telling myself it was gone or getting better. I had air fresheners all over the car, trying to smother the stench, but every time someone else got in, it was the first thing they mentioned.

One day, I had a flat tire. I pulled over, popped the trunk and began to remove the spare when I noticed something down in the wheel well. The edge of a small, brown paper sack was just visible. As I pulled it out, I discovered the package of hamburger meat we couldn't find at the cookout. Obviously, it had fallen into the spare tire well after I went grocery shopping. However it got there, there it was, sitting down in the wheel well, blasting out an odor that could put you back on your heels.

The only lesson I learned at the time was to search more thoroughly for any suspicious smells in the future. But, many years later, as I was being considered for managing partner of HORNE LLP, a professional services firm, this experience with rotting hamburger meat took on a new meaning.

I remembered how I drove around in that car for weeks, trying mightily to convince myself that it didn't reek. I was adamant that it was getting better. Years later, it struck me that the same could be said about countless companies and organizations when it comes to their culture. Ask almost anyone in leadership about the culture where they work, and most will tell you they have good culture. It's all too easy to go on for years thinking we have a good culture that is pleasant, engaging, and getting better and stronger when the truth is anything but that.

The dynamics are also important, as even solid cultures can get smelly over time. What makes it hard to spot is that deteriorating culture comes from chronic problems, not outright emergencies. It's easy to respond to emergencies—saving the star employee from leaving, changing a policy the team is upset about, trying to catch up to the market on salaries, going remote due to a pandemic, throwing together a memo on a policy change.

But chronic problems can bring anyone down from good to smelly to simply rotten—slowly and insidiously.

That was the situation at HORNE around 2010–2011. In many ways, we had become so insular that we didn't recognize that our culture was not as good as we told ourselves. It was definitely not what we aspired for it to be. It was as though we were all riding in my Ford Falcon but nobody dared to say anything as we kept the windows rolled down.

GOOD ENOUGH JUST MIGHT NOT BE

Don't misunderstand. Many companies have good-enough cultures—by default. We had a good-enough culture at HORNE before starting our journey to build the Wise Firm—the name we chose for the culture we were working to create. Our founders, specifically Roy Ward, had provided us with a great vision and a solid foundation of core values.

Honoring God and our people were foundational elements that Roy helped instill in our firm. Gratitude and prayer were and are still today key components of our partner meetings. Frankly, the only reason we have a story to share with you is that we can speak from the solid foundation that our founders built. As our story of building the Wise Firm culture unfolds, it's clear the coincidences of God, faith, and culture began in the very founding of our firm. They weave their way throughout the entire Wise Firm journey.

If you talked to people on the street, if you chatted with others in our profession, they would all have said that HORNE was a good place to work. We had all the right sayings and slogans. We preached diversity and inclusion. We certainly met many people's expectations, and from the curb, we looked inviting. To top it off, we were very successful financially. And you try not to rock the boat when you think you're doing well.

But while who we were and what we did were certainly admirable in many respects, we also had our share of issues. There was no real unity in the partner (ownership) group. Our team members' experiences were inconsistent; many were downright bad. We had areas in the firm that were borderline toxic, as was evidenced by our excessive turnover. In some instances, the leadership was destructive. We were seeing unsettling evidence of some client churn. Our client experience was inconsistent. Although you could hear partners and managers shouting "client service" as our rallying cry and purpose, we were not a consistently high-performing organization.

Overall, people felt like they were just tools in the system—a human plug-and-play tool. Their dreams, what they personally aspired to, were not necessarily a focus of the firm or their leaders. Input was limited due to the all-too-common demons of fear and politics. Far too many people lacked a strong sense of belonging. Their personal connection to our purpose and firm was weak at best. Frankly, we were focused more on control than on people's dreams and full potential.

As Dr. Henry Cloud puts it, culture is what we create, what we are intentional about, as well as what we simply allow.[6] In our case, we were allowing too many of the wrong behaviors. It was culture by default rather than culture by design, and that culture was hindering our ability to serve our people and our clients. We hadn't necessarily planned to become what we were, but we were there, nonetheless.

Our culture didn't serve everybody on an equal basis; it benefited some more than others. It was not distinctive in any way, and it wasn't leading to the sort of growth and high performance that many of us knew we were capable of. Our client experience was inconsistent and was missing the *wow!* it needed; as a result, we had very few clients who could be described as enthusiastic cheerleaders. We were bogged down in the comfort of a good-enough culture. It kept us from focusing on high trust and high performance with a strong sense of belonging—all hallmarks of truly great workplaces. Moreover, had we merely stayed the course and continued

---

6   Dr. Henry Cloud, *Boundaries for Leaders: Results, Relationships, and Being Ridiculously in Charge* (Harper Business, 2013).

with the default culture we had in place, we would have been badly positioned for the future.

Just look around you today at the exponential explosion of technology, the Great Resignation, and the war for top-tier talent. The culture that we had in 2011 would have been sorely challenged to manage those issues, let alone fully leverage the opportunity they carry. And given the increasing level of turnover that the culture was actually driving, we were draining our internal pipeline of future leaders.

Unfortunately, we weren't the exception in many ways. Our approach to culture and other issues was consistent in large part with the accounting profession and businesses in general. Looked at it in another way, our shared, brutal reality was that we were all 15-year-old kids driving around pretending that our cars didn't reek of decaying hamburger. And since we were just one of many, successful in many ways despite it, that made change even harder.

As I mentioned earlier, like many other companies, our most consistent rally cry was about client service. But it rang hollow in the ears of team members who struggled to feel valued, respected, or motivated to give that extra effort to grow something special. We were completely ignoring the fact that *why* we work determines *how* we work.

It's not easy to see good culture for what it is. We too often miss the frequent odor that limits our ability to reach our full potential as an organization. Fortunately, the partners of HORNE and our managing partner at the time—Dr. Hugh Parker—had the courage to face the brutal reality of our "good" culture. They displayed the uncommon discipline to embrace a vision to chase greatness with a daily journey that begins with a beBetter mindset.

THE WISE FIRM WITH MAGNETIC CULTURE

Our ultimate goal on the Wise Firm journey is to build a vibrant, diverse organization where everyone feels that incredible sense of belonging: *This is where I belong. This is where I can make a difference. I'm truly a member of this community, this tribe, this culture. My voice counts, and I can be me.* By leveraging the resulting positive and magnetic energy from our team members, we will deliver a client experience that is distinctive.

In fact, the commitment to a people-first culture is not only worth it, it's absolutely essential today. I wholeheartedly agree with Patrick Lencioni's teaching in his book *The Advantage*, that culture is the only distinctive advantage you can hope to maintain for the long term.

Magnetic cultures are great. Great cultures are magnetic. Cultures become a distinct advantage when they become magnetic. It begins to grow itself as more team members work to grow and protect it. Magnetic cultures are workplaces where people feel loved and cared for, where they have a strong sense of belonging and are appreciated for who they are and for the strengths they bring to the team. They know they are building something bigger than themselves. In great cultures like this, high trust develops through transparency. Magnetic cultures are transparent about where they are and what can be better. They measure and report on the progress to everyone. It's very difficult to build high levels of trust without a high degree of transparency. Communicate the *why* behind all initiatives and big changes.

Looking forward, as business models evolve at such a rapid pace and continuously transform with technology, a magnetic culture will be the only way to be creative, anticipatory, and relevant to both employees and clients over a long period of time. Companies that don't recognize this current reality will struggle to survive, let alone thrive.

I fully understand that culture, in the eyes of many, supplants a more important objective. For some leaders, the client is king; people and culture don't come before that. "Client first!" is a great rallying cry for short-term results. But that can be a very slippery slope, as it ignores the interrelated, complementary relationship between your culture and customer care. This is an apt description of where HORNE's good culture was positioned when our journey began to build something better. I would argue the opposite. How can a team member, consistently and over a long period of time, deliver client service with care and create *wow!* experiences if they do not believe the organization and leadership care about them?

The truth is that both culture and client service are critical for sustained growth and relevance. It's also true, regardless of priority, there will be client service failures and employees with bad experiences. It's simply unavoidable in an organization of humans. However, if we focus on people first as the top priority, then strong, energized teams who connect their purpose, their values, and their dreams will build a magnetic culture, a better company. They will deliver long-term, more consistent, and better client experiences while avoiding that slippery slope of turnover, disengagement, and leadership gaps. These pitfalls are more prevalent and destructive in organizations that drive client service to the detriment of building a great culture.

I'll be so bold to say that when leaders prioritize client service over their people, then when trouble arises, that bias toward clients will rear its head for everyone to see in negative and detrimental ways. Whether it's employee stress and burnout, missed deadlines, service failures, or something as simple as implementing higher production expectations, the interactions motivated by this mindset always lead to morale problems, higher turnover, less commitment, minimal effort, and overall mediocrity.

Great client service demands a culture where people feel valued, respected, and part of something that's meaningful. The stronger a sense of belonging is for your team members, the more consistently their client service will exceed expectations. I like to call it the *wow!* experience. What drives this elevation of commitment to client service and the company mission?

Great culture focused first on your people unleashes the all-important magnetic energy. This can be hard to measure, and if you've never had it, you won't know what you are missing. This magnetic and powerful energy comes from a strong sense of belonging, high levels of trust, positive morale, and an intrinsic desire to contribute and help build the culture. The defining moment is when leaders trust, believe, and recognize the inherent good in people. Magnetic cultures create the community, a tribe, a team that we all desire in our lives and as part of our work. People are thirsty for more meaning and purpose in their workplaces. This energy drives discretionary efforts, the mindset that we will run through a wall together. It breeds critical thinking, innovation, and teamwork.

When we have a strong sense of belonging, we care about our performance and our client service as our full potential comes into play. Our mindset moves from "have to" to "get to." Passion, pride, and loyalty are evident. Still another benefit of this magnetic energy is that it attracts more talent as your team members share the story about their culture. Magnetic energy is not only real; it is the game changer.

Our company, HORNE, is still on a journey. We haven't reached a particular destination; that's not the point. Our journey to becoming the Wise Firm takes place every day, as we actively build the kind of firm we want to be part of. We make caring and creating a sense of belonging for each other top priorities. Our core values provide us a compass that helps us move quickly and in the right direction.

Hard decisions are grounded in what is best for our team and our clients. Our thoughts, our words, and our actions shape our culture every day. Our purpose drives us forward together to serve our clients with excellence. HORNE has become a higher-performing organization propelled by a magnetic culture with better client experiences as a result of our journey.

In the words often attributed to Walt Disney, "Disneyland will never be completed." And neither will a great workplace culture. Instead, it will continue to change, grow, and evolve to be relevant; this is the beauty of a magnetic culture. Frankly, if companies viewed their culture as people first, they would experience more of the magnetic energy that may be hard to measure but that has tangible, positive results in performance, client experiences, and growth.

Nothing in this book should lead anyone to believe that a magnetic culture is perfect—far from it, as you will see in our journey. Cultures are composed of human interactions, and all cultures endure mistakes, problems, client failures, and the daily opportunity to beBetter. There are no perfect cultures, and you are not chasing perfection. You don't ever win the culture battle. You simply earn the right to play the next day with the huge advantage of magnetic energy on your side.

Lencioni explained that this type of culture is a distinctive competitive advantage. A meaningful journey, a journey of true significance, is one where you are stronger each day than the day before and are moving forward on your journey toward a magnetic culture. High-performing cultures can't be left to chance; you must be intentional every day. Moreover, they are worth it because they provide you with a powerful team delivering significance as they consistently *wow!* clients with care and service.

Still, this must begin somewhere, and for most, that journey begins by facing the brutal reality of our once-present culture, which will almost always be called "good." A good culture is certainly the biggest barrier to a great one. Good cultures thrive in our comfort zones. It's the status quo, with the legacy of our past success that allows us too many unintended consequences; you cannot form a magnetic culture without an intentional focus on people first.

Good cultures lack the discipline to call out and make hard decisions on behaviors that are not aligned with the values or vision. Good cultures usually have lots of rules and controls, especially around client service. Lone rangers who have influence from past client successes seem to be the exception every week, regardless of how they treat people. Good cultures have low to average team member engagement, and discretionary efforts are few and far between. Companies with good culture usually see frequent client experience problems, slightly increasing client churn, slow organic growth, if any, and certainly turnover rates of team members that constantly threaten not just growth opportunities but sustainability. Another way of thinking about good culture is that it rarely has an abundance of raving cheerleaders.

||||||||||||||||||||||||||||||||||||||||||||||||||||||||||||||||||||||||||||||||||||||||||||||||||||||||||||||||||||||||||||||||||||||

MAGNETIC THOUGHTS

"Whatever you do, work at it with all your heart."

—COLOSSIANS 3:23 NIV

"So whether you eat or drink or whatever you do,
do it all for the glory of God."

—1 CORINTHIANS 10:31 NIV

"Culture is not just one thing; it's everything. Culture drives expectations
and beliefs. Expectations and beliefs drive behaviors. Behaviors drive habits.
And habits create the future. It all starts with culture."

—JON GORDON, *THE POWER OF POSITIVE LEADERSHIP*

- Magnetic cultures are workplaces where people feel loved and cared for. They have a strong sense of belonging and are appreciated for who they are and for the strengths they bring to the team. They feel they are building something bigger than themselves.

- Magnetic cultures create a community, a tribe, a sense of belonging that we all desire in our lives and in our work.

- A magnetic culture also mandates transparency—the courage to accept difficult conversation as a central component of building trust and a sense of belonging.

- Great client service demands a culture where people feel valued, respected, and part of something that's meaningful. Client service is affected by how people work, which is driven by why they work.

- A magnetic culture is created by being intentional with a people-first mindset—trusting and believing in the good in people.

- A magnetic culture has no end point or final destination. It's always evolving and adapting to meet new challenges and leverage fresh opportunities.

- Magnetic cultures are great, and great cultures are magnetic.

- There are no perfect cultures. You're not chasing perfection.

- The greatest barrier to a magnetic culture is a good culture where we find ourselves clinging to the status quo, legacy success, and our comfort zones.

2

Unworthy:
The Wise Firm Vision

A LOT OF DEEP THOUGHT and prayer went into the Wise Firm vision to propel HORNE on a journey to creating a magnetic, people-first culture. God and faith and maybe a coincidence or two played important roles all along the way. The transparency of this chapter was one of my biggest challenges in writing this book. It reveals my mistakes and shortcomings as a leader as well as my growth. The intention of this transparency is simply to share the leadership lessons I learned that may help you on your journey. It was not a journey that I planned but one on which I was lucky enough to be there when it all happened.

In 2010, Dr. Hugh Parker announced he would retire from the position of managing partner at HORNE, effective May 2012. Dr. Parker's strong leadership the prior eight years had helped us achieve a strong growth pattern, increase our talent resources, and evolve into a more corporate governance entity. This decision-making structure provided us the ability to be more consistent across the firm, make decisions more quickly, and in many ways contributed to our ability to grow our firm. The entire partner group knew the selection process for a new managing partner would be our next defining moment. One question remained: Who would be our next managing partner, our leader?

Due to my long tenure with the firm and the fact that I had served as the leader of our two largest focus areas, speculation was rampant that I was a leading candidate. Of course, the thought had crossed my mind more than once. Obviously, I also heard this chatter.

At the time that we began the managing partner search process, I was the partner in charge of the government services group. I loved where I was and thoroughly enjoyed the relationships I had with others in that area of the company, along with our clients. Our group had been wildly successful in terms of growth. We had also built a very strong team to serve our government clients.

With all that in place, I was frankly unsure if I wanted to be the managing partner. On one hand, I was feeling selfish for wanting to skip the opportunity; at the same time, I wanted to go for it. On top of that, I truly wrestled with self-doubt. Accompanying the buzz about my candidacy was the issue of trust. Granted, the feedback was scattered, but the issue of others' trust in me kept cropping up. Although I later came to learn that the question of trust was due to the fact that many people didn't really know me, it was nonetheless heartbreaking and very troubling.

Not only did this hurt me, but it sharpened my doubt about whether I was worthy of this role. I knew in my heart I was not ready in so many ways. I felt an obligation to serve in that capacity, if that was my highest and best use, but gosh, I loved my work where I was.

All of the side conversations I was having with myself were frankly exhausting. I had no idea what I was going to do or really what I wanted to do. But I knew nominations were due by mid-February 2011.

Thank goodness for my good friend, partner, and fellow board member, Dee Boykin, who invited me to join him for a white-tailed deer hunt in Alabama in early January 2011. This was a great opportunity to get away from all of the managing partner confusion and just enjoy God's creation, some fresh air, and time with a great friend and his wonderful dad, Ollie. I knew some great fun stories, incredible meals, and a bourbon or two were waiting for me.

It was January 14, a bitterly cold but bright, sunny day. I had just crossed the Alabama state line from Mississippi. As I turned onto the two-lane blacktop road for the last stretch to the hunting camp, I was suddenly overcome with all the stress of standing for managing partner. Although I was doing something completely disconnected from work, it washed over me like waves over a breaker. I couldn't escape the crushing sense of unworthiness.

As my mind continued to race, I also lingered on critical feedback that some of the other partners in the company had expressed: As part of the chatter, several partners had made it plain that they did not trust me. Some thought I would be too demanding. To be honest, that lack of trust in me was absolutely crushing. It brought back memories of my first, very painful performance review with Arthur Andersen. I was average in every category but two. There, I was told I needed to improve even more. I had the same, hollow feelings years later.

Over the next several weeks, all of this caused me to truly doubt my ability to lead an organization like HORNE. In a way, it was odd—feeling so low and insecure at a time when you might be asked to fulfill your biggest role and responsibility yet.

Before I knew what was happening, I pulled over on the shoulder of the road and started crying. I wept uncontrollably as all of this pressure, anger, disappointment, and doubt clouded around me like a heavy fog. I told myself I didn't want this huge responsibility. I reminded myself that I was very happy in my present role. I was successful. I didn't need this, and I knew some of the partners didn't want me. Why risk all that by pursuing a job that I myself suspected I wasn't suited for?

In the middle of this emotional tumult, I went back to where I should have been the whole time. I prayed. *God, I have no idea what to do or what You want me to do. I'm not sure why we are at this crossroad. Am I even capable of leading in this role? Is this Your will? I know I can't do it without You. Is this what You want me to do?*

I asked for clarity and vision. As it says in Deuteronomy 8:18, "But, remember the Lord your God. For it is He who gives you the ability to produce wealth."

Be careful about asking God a question like that unless you are very serious and very ready. At the time, I had no idea what God was going to do. But on the side of this rural Alabama highway, I turned the question of my future role over to God. I pulled back onto the road, feeling better but still very much unsure what my future direction would be.

To draw my attention away from my worries and confusion, I began to focus on spending time with Dee and his father and the joy of being out in nature on a bracing winter day. I didn't put two and two together back then, but on this trip, I killed one of the biggest bucks that the club where we hunted had ever harvested. It's a beautiful trophy that hangs in my cabin at Willow Break in Mississippi today.

Looking back, it certainly provided personal confirmation that I might be headed in the right direction in my new role. At the time, I just discounted it as pure luck, simple coincidence. But let's just say our journey is full of coincidences. God, faith, and culture just kept intersecting and pushing us all forward toward the Wise Firm.

I've also come to appreciate that those sorts of feelings about taking on new responsibilities and leadership issues are not only normal, they're healthy and absolutely essential. With any big opportunity, it's human to feel unworthy, unready. We all often cling to where we are or simply fear the demands. Too often, we allow these feelings to hold us back, to make us hesitate. If we do not face them, they can prevent us from reaching our full potential. As I learned, it is far better to be candid about all your doubts and misgivings, because that's the only way to address them.

This applies to all leaders but particularly to those who are taking on significant responsibility for the first time. It's one of the obstacles that I see newer, less-experienced leaders struggle with. Encouragement is so important to grow those leaders of the future you so desperately need.

As mid-February approached, I was informed that I had been

nominated to stand for the managing partner role. On February 15, I went to Memphis to meet with James Gordon, a partner in the firm in charge of our public and middle-market focus area. I respected James's opinion and wanted his advice on what to do. I shared with him that I planned on putting my name in the hat. I expressed my frustration at the informal feedback that had made its way to my doorstep—the lack of trust and worries that I would ask too much of everyone.

When I asked him for his insights and advice, James said that, based on his own inquiries, those who had their doubts about me really didn't seem to have a specific reason. As he saw it, they just didn't know me very well. They had no idea what my vision or expectations were. They didn't feel connected to me.

He encouraged me to stand for election. He then gave me the advice that I needed to hear. To build trust, he said, you have to face reality. Their perception is your reality. He urged me to go meet one-on-one with all of the partners—each and every one, one at a time. He said I should listen to what they have to say. This was another life lesson that we are better leaders and grow faster toward our full potential when we listen to the advice and feedback of those who care about us.

The February 21 deadline came. I accepted the nomination and subsequently threw my name in the hat. Ultimately, 12 different partners received nominations. When the dust settled a week later, only five of us had agreed to stand for election. Over the next two weeks, we were to perform self-assessments and review the role and responsibilities of the managing partner. During this short period of time, three more partners decided to withdraw. Now, we were down to two.

Meanwhile, I followed up on the advice James had offered me. As he had suggested, I took the time to meet individually with every partner in the firm—roughly 40 or so. Even though I recognized the advice as sound, I dreaded every one of these meetings, terrified of what I might hear. While I hoped they would get to know me better, I was primarily focused on truly listening to what they had to say—what they saw as the future of the firm and how they felt about the possibility of my leading the company. I asked for feedback on what I could do better. (Asking for feedback is a leadership practice I must continue to work on so that I can grow as a leader.) I didn't offer any projections; I was there to listen and ask questions, and that's all I did.

Those were invaluable meetings in many ways. It gave me the opportunity to personally connect with each of the partners. But just as important, if not more so, their observations and thoughts became the backbone for the vision for the company's future—the vision that eventually evolved into the Wise Firm. The partners were honest and forthright in their remarks, and I will be forever grateful for what they shared. I had rebounded from my roadside meltdown. I could feel my confidence rising as I listened to each partner. Every direction I turned, God seemed to be leading me forward into this role.

Then the next storm hit.

On March 31, both candidates were evaluated by the partner group covering a variety of skills, strengths, and weaknesses. To be blunt, the feedback was brutal and specific:

"I don't trust Joey."

"Joey is too much like Hugh."

"Joey wants to fix something that isn't broken."

And on it went. As I said, it was a brutal experience for me. My business partners—who I cared deeply for and whose feelings and opinions I took to heart—had cut me wide open. I felt exposed. My pain was deep and genuine. It dragged me back to feelings of anger and uncertainty. Was all this really worth it?

As tears flooded my eyes, I felt hurt, unappreciated. It made me fighting mad one moment and a coward wanting to run the next. It felt as though I was being held to a standard I didn't see anyone else living up to. It seemed so unfair. I truly felt like I was a failure. I'm not sure I have ever felt so alone.

That feedback helped me embrace reality. The problem was me, not the other partners. I had not spent the energy and time to connect to others. I had operated too much as a lone ranger, seeking forgiveness over permission, so to speak. I realized there were opportunities where I could have elevated others rather than chasing a goal myself. I understood how I could be viewed as selfish or too driven, and I was. As an introvert, I had not openly shared how much I cared or who I was deep down inside. It was again an awakening that I needed.

Still, it pulled me back to my experience during the hunting trip. Was I really the right person for this job?

Once the emotion of the moment had passed, I began to realize that I had been presented with an enormous opportunity. However candid the feedback was, I came to understand that it would make me a much better leader, as well as a better person. Frankly, I needed that kick in the rear. I was too confident and had developed those blind spots that hold us back from our full potential. It refocused my attention on the value of honest self-awareness and the opportunity to leverage all that I had heard to improve myself in any number of ways.

I began to work diligently on the notes from my individual partner meetings. The partners had provided me with so many insights into what was smelly about our "good" culture and how we could improve. They communicated a desire and vision that we could be better. Here, again, faith intersected culture as I prayed diligently for God to provide me the vision we needed to be the firm He wanted us to be.

On April 22, I was informed that the other managing partner candidate had withdrawn his name. Now there was only one—me. I guess God was laughing at the clarity He had brought to my prayers. Another coincidence? This actually increased the pressure, as I knew it was imperative to have a unifying vision to move us forward during what I anticipated would be a period of accelerating change and challenges for our firm and profession. It's never healthy when trust issues, a lack of unity, and self-interest infect your partner group. Add to that disruption knocking on the front door, and it was clear that a compelling vision was critical.

BIRTH OF THE WISE FIRM

During these times of meditation, prayer, and creative thinking, the Wise Firm vision was born from the biblical parable of the wise man and the foolish man. You can read the story in the book of Luke, chapter 6, where the wise man built his house on the rock and the foolish man built his house on the sand. The storms came, the winds blew, the rain pelted down, and the foolish man's house washed away. But the wise man's house stood firm.

In my heart, I felt God was calling us to build the Wise Firm, a firm built on a solid foundation of *we and service*, a firm with a strong sense of belonging for everyone while having a focus on the future, not the past. We'd be a firm overflowing with positive energy! But frankly, I was also scared! Remember, be careful what you ask God for. It's scary when you think you might be getting close to a compelling vision. In fact, it *should* scare us. Do you feel frightened when considering your vision for culture in your company? If you do, you're probably on the right track.

I had the big picture vision. Now what? As the transition process moved along, I was tasked by the partners with developing a presentation with which I could outline my vision for the company. That presentation was slated for a town hall meeting of the partners, where we would all gather together as one to hear and consider a vision with which we could move the company into the future. This introduces our next champion in our journey—Dr. Joe Paul.

Joe was my personal career coach earlier in my career, and he was the perfect choice to work with me to prepare for the most important presentation of my life. He had already helped me to grow as a person and a professional, and he knew our firm very well. We began an intense practice session schedule for my presentation to the partner group. God bless him for the patience and discipline to endure those demanding run-throughs. We practiced the Wise Firm vision by my building a Wise Firm and a Foolish Firm side by side. The Wise Firm was built on the foundation of *we and service* compared to the Foolish Firm built on *me and self-interest*. We went block by block until we reached the top, where positive energy opposes negative energy.

Then it happened. I came very close to making a critical mistake that could have undercut God's plans for our firm. Two days before the presentation, Joe and I were in our last practice session. I told Joe I wanted to tighten up the presentation and felt the Wise Firm was too "out there" for us. At the time, it just seemed too radical.

Now Joe is usually very reserved and methodical in his feedback. He immediately stood up and glared at me. "Joey," he said, "you are not going to throw out the Wise Firm. It is the heart of your presentation. It lays out the vision for the future. No, you cannot drop the Wise Firm." So, for the rest of our story, remember that I'm the guy that tried to throw out God's vision for our firm. Joe Paul is the champion who saved it. It was certainly not a moment that I am proud of, but again, at the intersection of God, faith, and culture, God continued to move us in the right direction in spite of me. Another coincidence, I'm sure.

May 5 arrived and, with it, the birth date of our Wise Firm vision. The setting was the town hall partners' meeting. With only one candidate remaining—me—I would share a vision for the company moving forward. Part of my presentation consisted of two large boards, each of which contained information and thoughts gathered during my individual partner meetings. One board was titled "The Wise Firm," and the other, "The Foolish Firm." As Joe and I had practiced, I placed different building blocks under each. From there, I described behaviors that would likely be found in a Foolish Firm, such as constant blaming of others, looking backward all the time versus looking forward, and pervasive negative energy. I did the same for the Wise Firm.

Here's the complete breakdown:

FOOLISH FIRM	WISE FIRM
Me and self-interest	We and service
Rearview mirror view	Windshield view
Politics	Collaboration
Internal focus	External focus
A sense of competition	A sense of belonging
Transactions	Relationships
Backbiting	Forward thinking
Procrastination	Hard decisions
Talk about values	Honoring values
Lots of structure	Lots of flexibility
Making excuses	Getting results
Rigid decision-making	Empowered people
Lots of data	Lots of positive energy

As I spoke, I could see the partners shifting in their seats. It was resonating. We all knew that the company was riddled with politics, that there was a great deal of distrust, a lot of negative energy.

By contrast, the Wise Firm was completely different. The Wise Firm was driven by positive energy. There was a sense of unity and common purpose. The Wise Firm lived by the commitment to constantly improve. I asked the gathered partners: Where do you think we are? Is it genuinely where we want to be? Are people constantly looking to blame others? Is there a lack of transparency? How much do we talk about our past as opposed to how often we talk about our future? Why is our client experience average at best?

The contrast of who we really were with who we aspired to be was stark. The energy of the Wise Firm building blocks resonated. Now we knew our starting point and where we wanted to go.

The power of this exercise was to help everyone truly visualize where we were and the direction we wanted to follow. Another goal was comparing what we wanted to leave behind to pursue who we aspired to be.

That also resonated with the group. As partner Kade Moody, who was to become a key player in the development of the vision that is the Wise Firm, noted, "The vision that he painted was the one we all desired and shared. It was a moment of reconciliation that healed all divisions across our partner group." Our attention was on tomorrow, not yesterday—possibilities, not culpability.

But my remarks didn't focus exclusively on my thoughts about the firm as a whole. That's where the additional visual of a fishbowl filled with fake minnows came into play.

The idea for the fishbowl came from another champion in our journey, partner Cathy Denman. During a conversation about the turmoil and anxiety I was feeling, she gave me some of the sagest advice I've ever been blessed to receive.

"Joey," she said, "you are in a fishbowl. People know you are one of the front-runners for the managing partner. I appreciate how and why you're internalizing this. But, when you clam up, people assume you think you have it in the bag or that their opinion doesn't count. When they see you talking with a partner, they think, 'Well, he cares what they think but not what I think.' You have to talk about this, and you just have to open up more."

So I did just that. A key element of my presentation was a fishbowl filled with fake minnows. Although the minnows weren't real, what they represented was. Based on the feedback I had received from the partners, each fish stood for an area that I knew I had to improve on to become the sort of leader the company both needed and deserved.

One by one, I pulled those shiners out of the bowl and discussed my areas for improvement as honestly as I could. I wanted to make it absolutely clear that I had heard what the partners had had to say and that I was taking their feedback to heart. I was owning my weaknesses and drawbacks in front of the entire group.

I was also determined to show that I was ready to commit myself to becoming a better leader, colleague, and person. That, and the fact that we were all in this together. Transforming HORNE for the better would require more than just the actions of one individual; it was going to take all of us, united in both focus and action.

Our values always show up in the fishbowl. Seeing is believing. How we honor those values is critical to any journey of excellence. Do the decisions of leadership reflect those values and their communications? Do the promotions and the rewards reflect team members who are living the values? Looking into the fishbowl, do leaders consistently demonstrate those values?

So many companies have beautiful values, people-first slogans, yet it's hard to see those values lived out every day. People only believe what they see leadership do. Enron touted the values of integrity, communication, respect, and excellence. They were so proud of these values that they chiseled them into marble. What did their fishbowl demonstrate?

What Cathy shared is incredible awareness for any leader. As you move up in leadership, it is less about you and more about the people you serve. They do see and hear your every action. When you visualize the fishbowl, walk all the way around it. Look in it and under it. There's nowhere to hide. Moreover, if feedback jumps in as well, it's there for everyone to see. Every action, every word, every inaction, every nonword, every smile, every frown—they're all on display. There's no hiding in leadership; you can be full of denial and blind spots, but everyone else can see it plainly. *Every leader swims or sinks in this fishbowl!* Thanks to Cathy for opening my eyes.

I made sure to temper my enthusiasm for building the Wise Firm with a dose of reality. However committed we were to creating the Wise Firm, it wasn't carte blanche. To a large degree, we would have to make do with the resources we had on hand, and everyone in the firm needed to understand and embrace that to foster sustained, long-term growth.

That's when I shared the story of my granddaddy Dowdle. My mom grew up in the 1940s, in the aftermath of the Great Depression. Times were still very tough. When she was a child, from time to time, my granddaddy would bring home a big, thick steak for the family. He would have Grandmother cook it and then put the steak in the middle of the table for him to carve. The steak juices would just run out and seep all over the carving tray. By now, all of the kids' mouths were literally watering.

Next, he would put a plateful of Grandmother's biscuits on the table—so light and fluffy they seemed to float over to your plate. Granddaddy Dowdle would break one open and dip it in the juices. His mouth full, he would preach about how delicious those juice-sopped biscuits were. "Oh my goodness," he would announce, "I believe that's the best I have ever tasted. I'm going to eat another one."

Of course, by then all the kids were doing the same thing.

The biscuits were amazing, but that wasn't necessarily the point. What Granddaddy was doing was getting the kids to fill up on those biscuits and juices before he dished that steak up. That way the steak would go further. He had learned to do more with less.

Doing more with less, I pointed out to the partners, was one of two critical themes for our sustained growth strategy.

After I finished my remarks, the partners excused Hugh and me. As I learned later, they quickly agreed that there was no need to go through the remaining steps in the selection process. After Hugh and I rejoined the group, I was elected unanimously. This again only confirmed the power of God and the intersection of faith and culture.

Jen Wilson of ConvergenceCoaching, who facilitated this event, shared her thoughts: "Coming into the meeting, my partner Jack and I hoped Joey's presentation would address the partners' concerns and at least 75 to 80 percent of the partners would rally behind the leadership change," she said. "The Wise Firm vision had all the essential elements and provided the partner group with a compelling vision. They saw the very best of what was possible in leadership and vision, and they responded to it with a unanimous vote for approval. It was like nothing we'd seen before or since."

Kathy Watts, our health care leader, contrasted the meeting with the prior year's gathering—a stark comparison.

"I was hopeful going into the meeting to hear Joey's presentation but apprehensive due to trust being so low. My desire was for us to be at least somewhat cohesive as we looked to the future," she said. "Boy, was I pleasantly surprised. God led Joey with a message and vision that I immediately loved and embraced! It was powerful and very motivational! The visual aid also gave it impact. We had something that resonated on so many levels."

That reaction, Kathy added, was shared by others.

"This had a foundation on biblical principles. Bold and not ashamed. That is who we are and what guides us to serve clients, our team, and our communities. It was such a breath of fresh air," she said. "For me, it was so easy to embrace. The whole firm felt the same way. The partner group now had something to bond with. And so, it really helped unify us. For the first time, I truly felt I belonged!

"It was clear God was leading us in this direction."

Looking back, it was a critical step in beginning to build the Wise Firm. Clearly, the partners had the courage and discipline to face reality. We all embraced the value of a compelling vision and strong culture, but we also recognized that we simply didn't want to be like every other CPA or professional services firm on the block. To paraphrase Henry Ford, while other companies might be satisfied with a faster horse, we wanted the power and innovation of an automobile, something well beyond the status quo.

We all hit the ground running, starting with a commitment to establish and build on a policy of consistent transparency. Working closely with Kassi Rushing, HORNE's communication director, I began to write an internal blog to help the entire firm get to know me better, to share important elements and ideas, and, every bit as important, to reinforce the message that the changes we were looking to achieve required everyone's energy and enthusiasm. The blog proved so useful that we transitioned to a publicly distributed blog in 2014 (available at Joeyhavens.com).

In fact, Kassi was the key architect in all of our Wise Firm messaging. Her creativity and ability to help visualize and bring to life our key messages were critical to our fast start and ability to continue progress on our journey. Having a dedicated communication director was a big investment by our partners, and, in my opinion, now standing on the other side of a transformation, it is both critical and a best practice. Culture change requires communication clarity, which helps keep all of the leaders on point and helps the entire organization connect the dots between vision and action. For instance, we used lots of visual communication tools to help people connect. It takes a person in a dedicated role to make certain that communication is both clear and compelling. You must over-communicate your vision, purpose, and strategic plan. Communicate, communicate, communicate.

We were also committing ourselves to building subject matter expertise that would be unrivaled. That would allow us to bring exceptional value and worth. We could collaborate with clients on changing needs and, as a result, create a better experience. We were looking to capture the power of sharp focus—something that we believed our clients and the marketplace were looking for.

It was decidedly a two-edged sword. It created a new energy, a real sense that we were going to be a different firm and were going to do business differently. But it also fostered anxiety and uncertainty. People were asking how this would affect them, particularly if they didn't work in one of our focus areas (even among some of the partners). What we learned very quickly was that any significant changes to the ecosystem or business model in an organization has huge ripple effects (or waves, in our case) throughout your culture. Change impacts you in ways you couldn't ever expect.

In fact, one partner, Kade Moody, was so concerned that he wrote me a long dissertation about why this was crazy and how completely misdirected it was. It was perfectly understandable why Kade was concerned. In identifying various areas of focus in our repositioning of the firm, we had eliminated the portion of the company Kade was in charge of. It's not difficult to picture his frustration and uncertainty about whether, in fact, he still had a place at HORNE. Kade recounted this as being one of the lowest points of his career. He said, "I really questioned if I belonged at HORNE."

As it ultimately turned out, however, Kade proved to be an out-and-out champion in our efforts to recraft HORNE. With the firm continuing to have growth opportunities in health care, we approached Kade about the opportunity to transfer into that area, where his extensive audit knowledge and skills were needed. Kade transferred into our health care practice in 2013.

The rest of the story belies Kade's initial apprehension. He ultimately became the leader of our health care assurance practice, credentialled as a fellow of the Healthcare Financial Management Association, an equity partner in the firm, and a member of the board of directors.

"I truly know that this was my highest and best use and my calling for this point in time," Kade says. "I know that HORNE was, is, and will always be my home."

Kade is undeniably one of our biggest champions. He swam across the lake of fear, disappointment, and anger to evolve into one of HORNE's key leaders today. Kade is helping grow a focus area that he did not even work in before our restructuring. His experience shows how a culture chasing greatness helps people find their highest and best use.

EMBRACE EMPLOYEE REALIGNMENT

However inspiring, Kade's story begs the question: Does your culture promote and help people find their highest and best use? This mindset provides a great outcome for anyone that needs to change roles. We openly promoted and encouraged team members and partners to change focus areas to fit their skill sets and highest and best use. We've seen more than 100 such shifts since 2012. We celebrated their realignment with the entire firm, noting the courage it took to seek their highest and best use. This alone helped us retain many key leaders and put them on a path toward their full potential.

I frankly regret that we did not highlight this or recognize it soon enough in our journey to better help those who were drowning by simply being in the wrong role. The disappointment that comes from losing great talent stays with you a long time. If only we had been better, faster . . .

We also made it clear that other big changes were on the way. But it was clear we were all gaining the courage and commitment to challenge the status quo—each and every one of us. To work toward creating the Wise Firm, we all needed to know that we would be bucking any number of traditional, conventional ideas and processes. Every voice counted. Our shared commitment and resolve would make us that much stronger moving forward.

By giving careful consideration to the future direction of the company, as well as the resounding support for and embrace of a new vision, we were all in by this point. I know I was. The sense of being unworthy, of doubting whether I was up to joining with my teammates in developing and implementing significant change, no longer weighed on me. I could feel God working within our firm to do things that we could not have even imagined.

I realized I wasn't in this alone. By honoring God and serving others, we had numerous leaders stepping up from every level in the firm. In fact, no one—certainly not me or any other leader you can think of—can accomplish meaningful change by him- or herself. It's a big, emotional journey to move culture from good to magnetic. Only when you have numerous leaders embrace the compelling vision can you make it through the swamp of doubt, fear, anger, disappointment, and weariness. The pace can be slow and even tedious at times. But, once again, it's not only possible but worth every step of the way.

Building the Wise Firm, like any magnetic culture, isn't and cannot be just about the leader. We could do this, but only if we did it together while seeking to honor God in our service. On the other hand, leaders and leadership teams have to be intentional about prioritizing culture—a people-first mindset. Our compelling vision was already generating lots of magnetic energy for our journey.

Yet, as with anything that is worth doing, we knew the road ahead would be a hard one. We were not wrong. The challenges just kept coming.

MAGNETIC THOUGHTS

"Trust in the Lord with all your heart
and lean not to your own understanding;
in all your ways submit to Him,
and He will make your paths straight."

—PROVERBS 3:5-6 NIV

"So neither the one who plants nor the one who
waters is anything, but only God who makes things grow."

—1 CORINTHIANS 3:7 NIV

"And who knows but that you have come to
your royal position for just a time as this?"

—ESTHER 4:14 NIV

• Magnetic cultures start with a compelling vision. A bold vision. A vision of building something bigger than ourselves.

- You will have moments where you feel unsure about yourself, and that's okay. It's better to be candid about all your doubts and misgivings, because that's the only way you can address them.

- Take the time to identify what aspects of your organization are destructive (characteristics of the Foolish Firm) and what parts are valuable (those elements of the Wise Firm). Every company or organization has both.

- The traits of a Wise Firm include these: a strong sense of belonging, a compelling vision, a we-over-me mindset, service to others, faith-inspired values, growing positive energy, transparency, flexibility, and empowered forward thinking.

- It's important to recognize that leadership is life in a fishbowl. Everything is on clear display for all to see. Leaders must swim in a sea of transparency.

- Leaders can only reach their full potential and pursue God's purpose with humility and by embracing feedback to beBetter. Asking for feedback is a leadership practice we all must work on so we can grow as leaders.

- Leadership is about serving others and making decisions for the greater good, which will certainly take you out of your comfort zone.

- Understand that every form of change—particularly sweeping change (business model, organizational restructure, leadership transitions)—has a widespread impact and ramifications on culture, and often in places you don't expect it.

- A magnetic culture encourages everyone to find their best and highest use within the organization. Remember to allow for this and to embrace realignment.

- Culture transformation is a long, exhausting yet rewarding trip. Don't expect things to happen overnight. Resistance will take many forms, and legacy beliefs and assumptions will slow your progress at every turn.

- Having many leaders who embrace the compelling vision will help you make it through the swamp of doubt, fear, and disappointment. Continue to honor God. Success is not only possible, it's worth the lessons learned along the way.

3

Mindset Matters

WHEN I FIRST OUTLINED THE vision for the Wise Firm to the partners at HORNE, I was understandably nervous. Much of what we were considering was a thorough rejection of the status quo, a groundbreaking effort to completely reshape ourselves. Now, with the partners on board in their commitment to pursue greatness, it was time to take the message to the entire company. That was the setting for our annual HORNE Leadership Summit in 2012, a gathering of more than 400 team members from across the company to discuss in detail the plans we had in store for the firm. (We have now grown to over 2,000 team members!)

When I had first raised this broad-ranging topic a year before with the partners, I had more than my share of misgivings and doubt—scared we might not embrace the challenge we were facing, nervous the focus needed to accomplish this revolutionary change would rattle too many of us, and unsure about the lure of complacency.

Happily, that was not the case. First, we gave thanks to God in a group prayer for His many blessings on our firm. I also prayed silently that God would open up our minds to see His Wise Firm vision. As I opened my remarks to the assembled team members, I was pleased and proud to report that the early results were encouraging. Our year-to-date organic growth at that point was 8 percent, the best in recent years and considerably better than the profession as a whole.

Our board had realized that we were just scratching the surface of our potential as a company. We needed to keep up our efforts to keep that growth going. We needed to clarify where we were and where we wanted to be. We needed a common mindset to unite us and cement the focus of the group. We needed to beBetter. And, to do that, we needed to alter perceptions and mindsets, to clearly convey the message that, while change can be understandably unsettling, we as a group needed to view change as both reasonable and constructive, not inherently extreme or intimidating.

It reminded me of the time when my family and I disagreed over how generous the tooth fairy should be. In my telling of it, it begins with me slamming the door on my way out of the house.

"We are not going to have the tooth fairy bring $5!" I announced over my shoulder. *There*, I thought as I headed toward the car. *I'm standing on principle on this.*

It all seemed so incredible. For days, my wife and I had been arguing over what the tooth fairy should leave for my son Brandon who, at this point, had a tooth hanging on by sheer faith. As it happened, our next-door neighbor had started all of this by raising the per-tooth neighborhood ante to $5. My wife thought that wonderful. I thought it ridiculous. One dollar was more than enough. To make matters worse, I was on my way out of town. No telling what my wife would do if that tooth dropped while I was away.

When I got home late that night, there was a note on the dresser: "Brandon's tooth literally fell out today. He has his tooth under his pillow. Please do the tooth fairy before coming to bed." Tired and distracted, I brushed my teeth and eased into bed. Then came the nudge.

"Did you do the tooth fairy?" my wife whispered.

Equally drowsy and frustrated, I rolled out of bed and checked my wallet—$103 total, three singles and a $100 bill. She wanted five, and I wanted just one, so I compromised, tucking $3 under Brandon's pillow. Mission accomplished.

I was up, showered, and out of the house before anyone else was awake the next morning to make an early meeting. Pulling into the Jiffy Mart, I ran in to get my usual Diet Coke and sausage and biscuit. As I pulled out my wallet to pay the $1.98 tab, all I saw was a single dollar bill.

The pieces came together instantly. I realized that I had inadvertently left $102 under Brandon's pillow—two singles but, instead of the third, the $100 bill! I could picture him, $102 in hand, pulling out all of his remaining teeth to leverage the payday to the fullest. Frantic, I called home.

"Honey," I began (now was not the time to be adversarial), "I accidently left $100 under Brandon's pillow. Can you get it for me without waking him?"

Yes, she could. And, in so doing, left an additional $3—the $5 amount she had wanted all along.

Thereafter, we left $5 every time the tooth fairy came to collect a new tooth. And I was thoroughly on board with it.

It was an important lesson about being open minded, about challenging perspective, beliefs, and assumptions. Initially, I thought $5 outrageous. One close call later, it seemed the most reasonable thing imaginable.

Our stubbornness can limit our ability to see not only what's possible but also what's both reasonable and constructive. At the beginning of the journey toward the Wise Firm, it struck me that we needed to undo preconceived notions and assumptions about what was truly possible for us to achieve.

Still, no matter how dire a company's situation, true change is hard, even if it's welcomed. Any chance to move an organization out of status quo thinking toward a beBetter mindset requires intense focus and accuracy. We knew we must create as much clarity for the Wise Firm vision as possible. We also knew we had to make it personal. To accomplish that, we focused the 2012 Leadership Summit keynote to address four key questions before casting the vision for culture:

- What are we trying to achieve?

- How are we going to achieve it?

- What is your role in this effort?

- How do you all stand to benefit?

Let's dig into each of these questions.

What Are We Trying to Achieve?

On the surface, what we were looking to achieve was relatively straightforward. However, it required a significant shift in mindset and getting to a point where the status quo was viewed as no longer good enough.

We wanted HORNE to be recognized as an example of excellence in everything that the company did. We wanted to deliver a distinctive and unparalleled client experience. We wanted to be known as anticipatory thinkers and thought leaders. We believed we would achieve meaningful growth year in and year out if we stayed focused on our people and our clients.

But to be clear, our growth would be a result of doing things right and doing the right things, not merely an effort to be the biggest, which is just part of the journey to greatness.

We envisioned a company that generated a magnetic energy where talent sought opportunities to join in and help build the Wise Firm. It would be a company whose clients would croon its praises to others, a company where everyone felt a meaningful part of the whole, a genuine sense of belonging and contributing. It would be a place where people were appreciated and recognized.

We wanted to be a team not because we worked together but because we were building a culture, a community together, something in which we would all have a hand. Harkening back to the story about the smelly Ford Falcon that I had as a teenager, we were going to rid the firm of any smell that might alienate both people and clients. We were going to build the coolest ride on the road.

Just like my old car, HORNE needed fresh air to be its very best. We were not going to be complacent and wait until we lost another talented team member or valued client. Complacency is smelly, rotten, and dangerous.

How Are We Going to Achieve It?

Getting there would be anything but easy, and we shared that truth with everyone. If being distinctive were easy, if pursuing greatness were easy, then every company on the planet would be doing it. We believed it was worth it, and we had already seen a new spurt in growth as we set out on our journey.

But the hard way also involved looking at our business model in an entirely different light and challenging certain assumptions that once might have been seen as entirely off limits. More specifically, we needed to turn away from measuring inwardly focused issues such as billable hours, realization, and utilization and toward focusing more on meaningful, significant indicators that portrayed how we were performing: People- and client-focused indicators had to be developed. We needed to measure what truly made us better.

To follow this challenging path, we would need to toss away our security blankets—legacy assumptions, key performance indicators, and the stereotypic fallback that "we'd always done it this way." And, to do that, we would have to do it all together, as one group united in both purpose and action.

What Is Your Role in this Effort?

I confessed to our team members that at that time, neither I nor the partners necessarily had a definitive list of what each person's role would be in this massive undertaking. But what we did know is that it would take involvement of the group as a whole. It would require input, collaboration, and committed feedback to move from good to great—to beBetter. Every voice counts!

We also knew the change would include new and different skills, and we knew we'd have to teach our people how to be successful in these new ways. Although the pathway forward wasn't yet a step-by-step plan, the most critical first step was in place. We had the buy-in of the partner group. They were champions of the Wise Firm and committed to our beBetter mindset.

They collaborated to shine the light to move forward, and we would lean on each other for every step that followed. One team, one direction!

How Do You Stand to Benefit?

"What's in it for me?" That's a question that every person asks themselves, especially when it's something of such scale. It was one we believed should be answered. We needed this journey to be personal to be successful, and we certainly needed each team member to see how they would individually benefit.

So, we told them how and what we believed they'd gain: security, naturally enough, for their careers as professionals, as well as for their families. In a time when security was hardly synonymous with survival in the corporate world, we wanted to be yet another exception to the rule. We would be intentional in helping create a strong sense of belonging for every team member. We'd create teams where every voice counts and where we were each part of building something bigger than ourselves. Being part of a high-trust and psychologically safe team, where everyone's contributions were recognized and appreciated. We wanted a climate where people didn't fear making mistakes.

And just as important, a commitment to beBetter also meant a commitment to working to reach our full potential—every one of us on an individual level. We all needed to be challenged each and every day and to meet every beBetter opportunity (which sometimes feel like roadblocks) with shared focus and energy. That didn't mean needless conformity; rather, we envisioned a framework in which every person could excel and contribute individually to the shared goal of all. We all needed to push ourselves to achieve our full potential—to enjoy both the challenges and rewards and to never look back even once.

Additionally, beBetter stood for being an engaged steward, not just for our clients but for the company itself. It meant providing opportunity for each other while building a firm that could be passed along to subsequent generations stronger than when we found it. That was and remains a very high, worthwhile calling.

This point in time called for a game plan to put this beBetter mindset into actual practice. Our board introduced a distinct pathway forward, starting with culture.

CULTURE MUST COME FIRST

There was no other way to phrase it: A culture that prioritized people had to be number one. Our people would lead and generate the magnetic energy to transform our firm. Culture would be our primary tool with which we could leverage beBetter ideals to build the Wise Firm. Citing Patrick Lencioni, author of *The Advantage*, all of the traditional, conventional ways to outsmart and outdo your competition were quickly going the way of black and white TV—utterly obsolete. In the future, the only real long-term advantage was culture—a powerful, fully engaged team that prioritized a healthy culture.

Compounding our urgency and focus on people were hard trends we identified in 2012 for our profession; they all converged for a perfect storm, resulting in a lack of talent for as long as the next 10 years. For our firm to grow, to create incredible client experiences, we had to generate the magnetic energy that would attract and retain talent. We would need this competitive advantage to generate exponential growth. Little did we know, a coincidence for sure, that the pandemic would turn this perfect people storm from a Category 1 hurricane to a landscape-clearing Category 5. The Great Reevaluation!

All this was related to our team in a compelling vision using the biblical parable about the wise man and the foolish man—the same story we had discussed in the partners' meeting a year earlier about the wise man whose house withstood a storm because it had been built on rock while the foolish man's home, placed on sand, was washed away.

In our case, we knew the storms were coming, and we wanted to build a Wise Firm that would not only withstand those storms but allow us to be distinctive and thrive amid the change and uncertainty. We wanted a magnetic culture so strong that every external client would be able to see it, feel it, and experience it.

THE BUILDING BLOCKS OF THE WISE FIRM

We quickly recognized that it was imperative to be as clear and thorough as possible to convey all that the Wise Firm encompassed. Accordingly, we used building blocks to help us see, communicate, and understand what new behaviors we would need to build the Wise Firm while being able to contrast them with behaviors that would slow us down.

Purpose

What would be the foundation of our Wise Firm? The foundation was our purpose—which we defined as *we and service* in our original launch. The purpose embodied our beliefs and values. It's why we exist.

As we communicated the meaning of *we and service*, it was hard to ignore the sharp contrast with the behaviors that undermine so many other cultures. These destructive behaviors were illustrated as *me and self-interest*. The sharp contrast was important. It allowed us to embrace beBetter in the form of a team effort and to prioritize our purpose of serving each other and our clients. Today, we express this foundation, this common purpose, as *deliver with care*.

Honoring Our Values

Close to our foundation of purpose, we stressed the building block of honoring our values as opposed to simply talking about them. When we honor our values, we use them to keep us pointed toward our true north in our decision-making. They influence our decisions and guard against drift. They provide accountability for everyone. These values go back to the inception of the firm in 1962. During our journey of building the Wise Firm, and in its current state, we have refined our core values to four to provide more clarity into who we are and how we live:

- God: We honor God and personal faith.

- Family: We are committed to serving our families.

- Service: We are passionate about the client experience.

- Gratitude: We are grateful for our blessings.

Gratitude is absolutely central to who we aspire to be. When we are grateful, we can't worry. It doesn't mean we are thankful *for* all things, as some are not so lovely, but be thankful *in* all things because God always has a purpose. Gratitude is a key value of a magnetic culture.

A Sense of Belonging

Creating a sense of belonging for each team member is certainly one of the major foundational building blocks for any culture.

Growing each person's sense of belonging is critical to building magnetic energy. Today, we know you cannot achieve an engaged, inclusive, diverse, and high-performance team unless every team member has this personal security. There's no magnetic energy if you don't have a strong sense of belonging.

IN PURSUIT OF NEW BEHAVIORS

At this point, we knew we had to identify a new, more effective set of behaviors. Furthermore, we needed to connect the dots and be specific. Part of the journey was being clear about what new behaviors we aspired to and how they worked together.

The essential components included these:

Focus on the External

We knew our client experience was driven too much by compliance and due dates. Our legacy key performance indicators were all focused on ourselves. We would begin to measure client-focused results, become anticipatory (defined as forward thinking in the original vision) in our client service as we pursued a *wow!* client experience built on great relationships and relevance.

Hard Decisions

Our transformation as a firm would inevitably involve tough choices. For instance, one of the hardest decisions would be what we would focus on for client service versus what we would not. One of the toughest decisions, yet one of the most critical ones in any important situation, is what you are not going to do.

Flexibility

We knew that our culture needed more flexibility for team members to integrate their personal lives and careers. Flexibility must be unique for each team member. True flexibility is so much more than the ability to do remote work—so much more that I have dedicated a chapter to this key building block of magnetic energy.

Collaboration

We knew that, for us to make this journey of transformation, we must move past false harmony and grow our skills of collaboration. Collaboration helps team members find their highest and best use, as well as providing clients with relevant insights. As you read further in the book, you will see our attempts to make collaboration a strength of the Wise Firm culture— not to mention our surprise when we discovered a hidden barrier that can be found in most organizations.

Emphasize Results

Results and accountability matter. We wanted better goals and more focus on getting things done. We wanted to celebrate our results together. Our focus priority moved to results for our clients.

Empowered Team Members

This building block was so important because it helped our team members see the benefits of growing the Wise Firm. When you have clarity of purpose, mission, and high trust, people can make decisions, and the entire organization moves at a faster pace. We stressed over and over that every voice counts. When people have a strong sense of belonging, they are empowered to take the risks that are necessary to pursue their full potential. It's amazing how these building blocks are so integrated in growing a magnetic culture and high-performance team.

Lots of Positive Energy

This is how we described the magnetic energy from making culture the number-one priority. When a team has a strong sense of belonging, provides flexibility, has a high level of trust, collaborates on opportunities, truly honors values, and pursues a common purpose, you are going to generate a lot of positive energy. As people make more choices to contribute and go the extra mile, that energy becomes magnetic energy that generates more effort, more growth, better talent, and more clients. It's pervasive on its own. If you take care of people and focus on your clients' needs, the numbers will take care of themselves.

More Fun

We also discovered as we began our journey that we were having a lot more fun. That's a remarkably valuable dynamic. When people are having a good time doing what they're doing, they're naturally more energetic and enthusiastic. Fun helped fuel the magnetic energy we were looking to build.

The group's reaction was easy to spot, as it mirrored the one in the partners' gathering from the year before. When we discussed aspects and weak points that characterized the Foolish Firm, people could see the opportunities to beBetter. The visual of the Wise Firm building blocks and the aspiration of growing this culture together was motivating. You could feel the energy building in the room. It was an empowering, compelling call to action they were obviously responding to. They all knew that we all could beBetter.

These and other elements of the summit were a sweeping, comprehensive challenge to the status quo—both our own and those of our industry. We were all coming to understand that the objective of the Wise Firm was not to be the biggest one on the block but the one focused on people and high performance.

As with any big change, we had some distractors and doubters. Frankly, we had several partners who wanted to go a completely different route; they elected to leave the firm and pursue other opportunities. But we went to great lengths to frame that as constructively as possible. We believed in the path we were going to undertake, and if that didn't happen to align with someone's own personal path, we promised we would do everything in our power to support them in their pursuit to find another more suitable journey outside of the company.

Our vision was all about everyone reaching his or her full potential—about chasing greatness and purpose, about celebrating the sort of behavior and action we wanted to encourage. And if that, for whatever reason, didn't sit well with some, that was perfectly okay. It's far better to work for complete alignment from the very start.

In that way and others, the 2012 summit was pivotal in not merely sharing the vision we had for the company but in helping everyone begin to understand their role in that transformation. To move toward greatness, we needed to act as one in constantly challenging the status quo. Moreover, people needed to feel safe in doing so. A commitment to upending business as usual is crippled when those involved in the process don't feel supported and empowered. To beBetter mandated a courage borne of safety and support for everyone involved.

CULTURE SHOULD HAVE A NAME AND A VOICE

But what was perhaps the most compelling and powerful component of the strategic messages of the summit was our discussion of culture. And what made that particularly meaningful was that our culture had a name: the Wise Firm. Those three words said all that needed to be said. We weren't "committed to excellence" or "pushing the envelope" or some other hollow, vague phrase. We were going to build the Wise Firm, and we were all committed to making that culture come to life, day in and day out.

Together, we were building something bigger than ourselves and something that we could aspire to every day. The vocabulary matters when telling a compelling story. With a name, the story was that much easier and more effective to convey to everyone. Most importantly, it made our story easier for every team member to share with new team members, recruits, clients, and prospects. It was concise, on point, but no less meaningful. The story matters, and the name creates an open window of opportunity to share. This is our community, our tribe, and each of us has made the choice to be part of it and to help build it.

What echoes down your hallways, across your Zoom meetings, into your client meetings? Make the words that describe the company culture a mantra. Use the mantra with every audience—from employees, customers, and investors to the public. Put the firm's cultural values front and center. The very process of hammering out repeatable language will help associates align with the culture and the actions required to achieve and sustain it.

We also went to great lengths to make certain that all of the discussion about the Wise Firm at the summit didn't devolve into little more than mere talk. We needed to have a game plan to make certain that we could begin building and reinforcing the principles of the Wise Firm right out of the gate.

References to the Wise Firm started appearing everywhere—beBetter posters in the conference rooms, beBetter stickers at teammates' desks and workstations. Not just a visual, beBetter became part of our everyday vocabulary. It became a part of how we talked, how we interacted with each other, and how we thought about and worked with our clients. Never underestimate the impact of visual aids and shared language when transforming your culture. They are powerful.

I closed that year's summit with a parable involving football. I asked the team to try to recall someone we've all inevitably seen at all sorts of sporting events. In between chugging beer and cramming hot dogs into his mouth, he's busy yelling at everyone within earshot—the coaches, the players, even the cheerleaders. The reason, of course, is that he knows it all and wants to "help" all these misguided people on the field.

But there's a serious disconnect at play. However much he thinks he wants greatness, the loud-mouthed fan isn't willing to do anything meaningful to achieve it. The coaches and players will work to improve and, with luck and determination, will get better moving forward. Yet, despite all his wisdom, our fan will forever remain on the sidelines, yelling a lot and accomplishing nothing.

"As we leave today, let's put down our beer and hot dogs; let's put down our comfort zones, our excuses, our fears!" I concluded to the group. "Let's throw away jealousy and selfishness. Let's run down on the field and embrace these initiatives, embrace each other, embrace the challenge to be better. If we do that together, we will win together. We will beBetter."

INCLUSION IN THE JOURNEY

While our commitment to beBetter was beginning to take concrete shape, we also knew that we had many other areas of the firm that presented opportunities for us to move toward becoming a high-performing team. We realized that we needed input from our team members to understand what was most important to them. How could we learn more about our brutal reality so we could work on it together? How could we make this a regular process, built with high trust, a safe place to provide us direct feedback on how to beBetter?

These questions led to our formation of beBetter teams, essentially employee focus groups designed to help navigate the varied issues the company faces and to develop strategy based on the input of a number of people rather than just a few. Although the initial beBetter team members were selected to participate, the process later evolved to an application process. You could nominate yourself or someone else for beBetter team membership. It became really competitive. People wanted to be on a beBetter team. It was considered an honor.

We were also very intentional and transparent with the entire firm regarding beBetter teams. We communicated what the teams were working on (a board-assigned strategic focus), who the team members were, and the recommendations that came from the groups. We celebrated their solutions and demonstrated our appreciation with recognition for their personal choice to be vulnerable, to be creative, and to collaborate with a beBetter mindset.

One of the earliest changes made as a direct result of input from the beBetter team was a total overhaul of the new hire onboarding experience, specifically orientation. We shifted to a mandatory, in-person, two-day session that placed particular emphasis on the culture we were developing. It was an expensive shift in practice but one that clearly contributed to the success and growth we've enjoyed. This brought consistency in our messaging across all of our focus areas and really started a feeling of unity that helped people find a sense of belonging more quickly.

BeBetter teams reflected our emphasis on involving as many people as possible to take on pressing problems and challenges. True to our evolution toward empowerment and autonomy, they represented the company's recognition that leadership cannot—and should not—solve every possible problem, a misstep that far too many companies make. Instead, beBetter teams showed that answers were always there for the taking, so long as somebody knew to ask the question. BeBetter teams unleashed the power of the team with input and creativity provided from a very diverse group of team members. Today, beBetter team alumni can be credited with influencing strategic changes to recruiting strategy, training processes, and even adding new lines of business to the firm, just to name a few.

By wrapping up with that group commitment to beBetter in building the Wise Firm, we made certain that the summit would be more than just words. We were ready to hit the ground running. And I urged the group to keep their sunglasses handy, because the future looked awfully bright. However, it was also apparent that, although the sun was shining, we could also see some dark clouds coming our way.

MAGNETIC THOUGHTS

*"Let us not become weary in doing good, for at the
proper time we will reap a harvest if we do not give up."*

—GALATIANS 6:9 NIV

*"Don't be anxious about anything; but in every situation, by prayer
and petition, with thanksgiving, present your requests to God.
And the peace of God, which transcends all understanding,
will guard your hearts and your minds in Christ Jesus."*

—PHILIPPIANS 4:6-7 NLT

- Our stubbornness can limit our ability to see all options. It's important to undo preconceived notions and assumptions so we can see a new way forward. Practice challenging our own assumptions and beliefs first.

- We started our change by asking four key questions:

  » What are we trying to achieve?

  » How are we going to achieve it?

  » What is your role in this effort?

  » How do you all stand to benefit?

- Culture is everything. In fact, it's so everything that every culture should have a name and a voice—not just a catchphrase, but a name that embodies the vision or community, a mantra that everyone can voice and share. Vocabulary matters.

- We built the foundation of our Wise Firm culture on *we and service.* Later, we converted this to our purpose: *deliver with care.*

- It was valuable to encapsulate our mantra, our daily challenge, with the term *beBetter*. Find a phrase that harnesses what you're trying to accomplish to help everyone truly get what is happening and why they want to be a part of it. One team, one direction.

- To achieve clarity and truly live—and honor—our values, we refined them to focus on four: God, family, service, and gratitude.

- To move toward greatness, we needed to act as one and ensure everyone felt safe at work—empowered and supported—in doing that. Forming beBetter teams was an important step in that direction. Every voice counts.

- Culture change required a new approach to onboarding new hires, with emphasis on the culture. By understanding individual needs, we focused on helping new hires quickly feel a sense of belonging.

4

Be Flexible

AT THIS POINT IN OUR journey to build the Wise Firm, we had a great deal working in our favor. Our thinking about what was going to happen and our why were coalescing. Enthusiasm and magnetic energy were starting to build.

But, at the same time we were starting to measure more metrics of culture, we took a deep breath and looked up. All we could see was a huge roadblock called "flexibility." Our profession—CPAs, accountants, consultants—had a well-earned reputation of having very little leeway in where, how, and when people worked. What mattered were the hours. In the office or at a client's, hours worked in a year was a badge of honor. They were a sign of commitment and promotion criteria. But overtime and a lack of flexibility were causing serious problems with retention, especially with women. The causes were the culture killers commonly known as control and a lack of trust.

How could we possibly meet what seemed to be the overwhelming challenge of promoting complete flexibility in a profession where the lack of flexibility was notorious? One strategic step was our meeting with all partners and managers to demonstrate how our hands were tied if we all didn't buy in.

It's understandable to assume that flexibility refers to the issue of remote work. With the pandemic, remote work has jumped forward in adoption by at least five years as nearly every organization is providing team members with the option of some remote work. However, remote work or working from home is simply one piece of the puzzle, perhaps the border pieces of a big jigsaw puzzle.

The overall puzzle is true flexibility. It also includes the ability to choose when and how we work, not just where, and when to accelerate careers and when to let off the gas to prioritize other areas in life. Accordingly, we went right to the middle of the puzzle to look for solutions to empower our team members.

Admittedly, we were already out in front of the game compared to where our industry and professional service firms as a whole were prior to COVID-19. In 2013, we were already viewed as "progressive" because we had established policies for work balance arrangements that provided more flexibility than some other firms. Still, they were words on paper and a long way from meeting the actual needs of our team members. People needed to be empowered to manage their career and personal life. Our board recognized this as key to improving our recruiting and retention of great talent. It was particularly critical to the careers of female team members. We anticipated true flexibility as making our culture distinctive and empowering, and by providing our team members with trust first, we would build more trust in our culture. We forecast a perfect storm in the coming years, resulting in a shortage of talent, and if we could solve this barrier, we could generate exponential growth. However, we did not have a clue how to solve this dilemma.

FEARLESS, UNRIVALED

We knew that, to truly achieve the goal of beBetter, we would have to introduce precedent-shattering changes that focused on freedom, flexibility, and ongoing communication rather than mere rules. The ultimate path forward began with a firm-wide collaboration and a crowdsourced, team member–written philosophy that replaced all prior existing policies.

To reiterate: We got rid of all our policies intended to legislate flexibility. Instead of formal guidelines having to do with career balance and the like, we instead emphasized empowerment, autonomy, and freedom of choice. To summarize the philosophy in a few words, we were less concerned with the specifics of how people did their jobs and much more focused on results and outcomes. We also came to acknowledge that true flexibility would be unique for different teams and for each individual team member. We called it *fearless, unrivaled flexibility*.

Again, it just made all the sense in the world. For one thing, who knew better what they needed to succeed and excel at their jobs than the people doing them? Moreover, we realized it would be impossible to develop a great culture if people were not empowered to manage their own lives. This new philosophy was so bold and game changing that the board was rightfully concerned about our execution of this initiative while keeping client service at a high level.

However exciting our new approach to flexibility and the many other changes were, we knew we might ultimately encounter a common problem—great enthusiasm and action from people at the top and great excitement from those on the front lines, only to lose that momentum as people in middle management lacked understanding and commitment, resulting in misaligned actions that would hinder our progress. We had tons of data and information, but we also knew there were pockets in the company in need of dedicated attention.

As I like to say, things get done one conversation at a time. So that's what we set out to do. Realizing how important buy-in was from our partner group and managers, we arranged small meetings with all the managers and partners across the firm, in every location. We wanted to dive deep into why this was the right course for us. We communicated all of the long-term benefits of having real flexibility in our firm. At the time, little did we know that this alone would be a huge factor in our immediate success with client service during the COVID-19 shutdown in 2020—another one of those coincidences that had us on the right track. As the old Yiddish adage has it, *Mann tracht, un Gott lacht* (Man plans, and God laughs). Thank goodness that, once again, He was in control.

I personally led each session. We wanted all of our management team to understand the significance this would have for our future success. Flexibility would be a game changer for taking our culture from good to great and fueling the will of our team to choose to be high performers, as they were also empowered to manage their lives.

These meetings lasted about two hours. They were very interactive and lively. They also gave me the opportunity to emphasize that, at the end of the day, just how well any new philosophy and policies actually worked in practice would come down to them—the people most directly involved. To illustrate that point, in every meeting, I sat with my hands tied together—literally, with a big rope—for the first hour. The point was the other people in the room—not me—would be the folks to make this all happen. Our future was in their hands, not mine. The rope was a visible illustration of how important a role each partner and manager played.

Common problems, challenges, and other pertinent issues were covered to solicit the broadest possible amount of feedback and guidance from the greatest number of people. We discussed best practices for implementation of our new fearless, unrivaled flexibility philosophy. I subsequently realized one of the keys to these meetings was our transparency about how hard this was going to be. It was going to be painful. People would fail at their commitments. People would treat it as a right rather than a privilege earned by honoring our commitment to communication and client service. Some team members would go backward in results and growth. We knew people would have to learn the discipline and responsibility that comes with freedom.

LIVING TRUE FLEXIBILITY

We also knew that we would make lots of mistakes. I knew there would be dissenters in the room who would resist our new philosophy. One partner went back and told his team that this sounded great, but it would simply not work. About six months later, that led to one of those hard conversations where we "turned momma's picture to the wall" and had a real heart-to-heart on what that meant for the partner's future at our firm. Culture transformation requires hard decisions and a united front from leaders at all levels. Change will not come if you do not seek buy-in and are not forthright on what you allow.

Unfortunately, our anticipation of problems was very accurate. It certainly wasn't easy to live true flexibility; in fact, it was often quite difficult. Some team members and managers struggled with their newfound autonomy and flexibility. That's where the term *guilt vampire* came into play. It may seem hard to believe, but some teammates actually felt uncomfortable about exercising this new sense of freedom and flexibility.

Guilt vampires have always lurked around organizations. In particular, we noted that they had a huge impact on the retention of female team members. The feeling of some sort of "special deal" was causing a great deal of guilt, both self-imposed and guilt pushed by others. This had been a killer in our profession for years.

Happily, the choice of names helped shift mindsets. *Fearless* reflected our intentional efforts to kill the guilt vampires. We were encouraging every team member to be fearless in their pursuit of flexibility. *Unrivaled* was chosen because we knew very few organizations were truly implementing a flexibility philosophy that was driven by individual choice and commitment and measured on results. We saw this as a big competitive advantage, and it proved to be true as our recruiting efforts began to flourish with new talent coming to help build the Wise Firm.

We also emphasized that this wasn't a blank check by any means. We made it clear from the outset that this was a privilege, not a right. Furthermore, it was a privilege earned by honoring our philosophy of trust, commitment, and communication. Everyone had to do their part, and they had to have the results to show for it. For example, if you were working from home, you had to achieve the same results as if you were in the office. That you were working from home was not the issue in the least; what you were able to achieve was what mattered.

And, again, it took enormous courage to stand by the principle that flexibility meant consistent, no-holds-barred flexibility.

I remember one instance very early in this process when a partner sought me out to talk about a particular team member's interpretation of flexibility. It was one of those coincidences that ended up serving as a pivotal moment in our mindset shift about flexibility. This partner had asked his colleague why he wanted time off every Wednesday afternoon. With admirable forthrightness, the team member said that's when he was hoping to meet up with his buddies for their regular golf game.

However candid, the partner was clearly uncomfortable with the situation. "Was this really what we meant when we said genuine flexibility?" he asked me. The teammate wasn't taking his child to the doctor or caring for an aging parent or volunteering at a homeless shelter; he was taking his golf clubs to the course and volunteering to play 18 holes with his pals!

Our answer was blunt: The why didn't matter. The empowerment and results did. We realized, however, it was not our business to know the why; it was our job to manage client work and support every team member's unique needs. That didn't necessarily mean a blanket yes all the time. For instance, playing golf would be out if it precluded critical face-to-face time with a client. But, yes, we concluded, fearless, unrivaled flexibility meant letting team members do what they wished, so long as it didn't impact their professional performance or the performance of the team overall. And that included trying to correct a nagging golf slice, if that was the case.

Naturally, some team members struggled with communication, some with results. Although some in management took this as proof that the overall idea wouldn't work, support, encouragement, and candor helped overcome those doubts. Using a one-conversation-at-a-time approach, we urged management to stay the course, coached them on opportunities to move forward, and assisted with hard discussions on feedback to team members. We also reemphasized the fundamentals of our philosophy at leadership summits and state-of-the-firm presentations. We called team members out for being too lax on their commitment to client service while we celebrated individual team member success stories.

The message was clear: Flexibility does not mean less accountability. In fact, it boosts accountability, because more eyes are measuring results.

MORE THAN JUST "LEAVING EARLY ON A FRIDAY"

"When I started at HORNE, I didn't realize how much I could actually love the firm I worked for. I haven't been at HORNE long, but I have learned so much about myself, my profession, and my firm. I even vividly remember my first new hire orientation, HORNE FastStart. They told us that HORNE was big on flexibility, but that it wasn't a policy; it was a philosophy, and it even had a name—*fearless, unrivaled flexibility*. At the time, I didn't really understand what that meant. I assumed it meant that I would occasionally be able to leave work early on Fridays or that I could even leave work in the middle of the day to handle a personal errand if needed.

"I didn't really grasp how HORNE lives out the fearless, unrivaled flexibility philosophy until my dad passed away. When I lost my dad, I was devastated. I didn't know how to juggle taking care of my family and also taking care of my work responsibilities. At the time, I had only been with the firm for four months, so I was extremely hesitant about asking for time off or even just the help I needed.

"But I can't even begin to describe the relief and appreciation I felt when the firm and my team told me to take as much time as I needed. They were truly concerned about my well-being. I know this type of flexibility does not exist everywhere, and I will be forever grateful. When I came back to work, I was energized and had

continued

an increased sense of belonging. I was more than ready to give back to the firm that gave so much to me.

"This experience helped me understand that there are two directions of flexibility: flexing up and flexing down. As our executive partner Joey Havens says, 'Flexibility is a privilege.' Team members must have the same willingness to flex up as they do to flex down. And it's an equation of equal parts: communication + trust + commitment = fearless, unrivaled flexibility. That's what makes HORNE different. As I said earlier, I know not every company allows their team members the level of flexibility that I experienced. And you'll never catch me taking that fact for granted."

—Insights from HORNE team member blog

MORE CHALLENGES AND MISTAKES

There were plenty of missteps. In implementing a policy of flexibility and empowerment, we initially included a time-keeping component. Although the idea behind it was to measure work efficiency, many people quickly pushed back against it, calling the practice an uncomfortable form of "big brother" oversight and intrusion.

They were absolutely right. It completely ran counter to our stated philosophy about trust, communication, and empowerment. It took less than a week for that stark contradiction to slap me squarely across the face.

I knew I had to own it. We immediately called a teleconference with the entire firm. I simply told everybody flat-out I had made a big mistake. We were going to do away with time tracking on flexibility and get back on the path we knew we should have been on the entire time.

The brief implementation of a system to track flexibility was a big miscalculation but one that proved very useful—another coincidence. First, watching the head of the company readily admit to that sort of mistake in a highly visible forum actively demonstrated the message that transparency was the rule, not the exception. And that went for everybody. Second, it was also a moment that encouraged us, because we recognized that the pushback came from team members with a strong sense of belonging and sufficient trust—enough trust that they were willing to be vulnerable and provide us with beBetter feedback. They understood that every voice counted. It was a serendipitous experiment that measured authentic progress.

Flexibility was an ongoing struggle but well worth the effort. Ultimately, it all came together. Measuring results year to year, we started the process with roughly 24 percent of the company's employees saying they had sufficient flexibility to manage their lives. A number of years later, that topped 90 percent! Can you imagine 90 percent of your team, including hourly team members who have federal restrictions on flexibility, reporting they felt empowered to manage their lives and careers? Yes, it was worth every conversation, every mistake, every stressful moment. It has paid huge dividends for our team members, our clients, and our firm.

THE WISE ENGAGEMENT METER

Things were certainly moving in the right direction. We had captured the spirit and focus of our mission in a simple, three-word phrase—the Wise Firm—that was fast becoming part of our everyday vocabulary. The spirit and action of fearless, unrivaled flexibility were beginning to take hold.

But additional practical steps were necessary to keep us moving in the right direction. And identifying our next steps began with an underlying question: If we were going to be shifting mindsets and introducing groundbreaking ideas, how were we going to know if we were making any real progress? The excitement around the company seemed to be mounting, but that gave us all very little insight into whether our progress toward remaking HORNE was truly taking hold. We realized we needed a way to measure our progress. More specifically, we wanted to know how engaged every single member of HORNE was in the overall effort to build the Wise Firm.

At the time, we did not have the luxury of countless software programs and other technology tools that could have aided our attempts to not only measure but understand our team's engagement. There were a few products on the market, to be sure, but they weren't relevant to our objectives. We needed something that was beyond an easy checkbox. Rather than assigning an arbitrary score or some other numerical value, we set out to create a tool that would capture the immediacy of the effort—to measure the mindset that individual team members were taking into their workdays and also a mechanism for sharing and repeating our messages for change.

So, we decided to build our own measurement tool: The Wise Engagement Meter was designed to capture engagement in the most intentional manner possible. The system involved team members logging in on a daily basis and then choosing one of a variety of ways in which they could engage effectively on that particular day. Their choices included the following:

- Make a difference. What can I do today to achieve real impact?

- Fulfill my purpose. What can I do to address what I feel is my true role?

- Feeling grateful. Do I take the time to remember all that I have?

- Collaborating. Am I doing more than merely cooperating?

- Proactively guiding. What can I do by choice to offer others direction?

- Serving. Do I remind myself that the highest goal is to serve?

- Focused. How locked in are we on the target?

- Feeling positive energy. Do I recognize positive energy and look to pass it along?

- Face-to-face. Do I take the time to focus on personal interaction—a critical step in building a Wise Firm?

- Smashing the day in the face. A fan favorite and an edit to the meter based on a persuasive submission from one of our rising stars: Do I emphasize what I need to do to crush what needs to be done in a particular day?

- Slaying the guilt vampires. A strange but an important one, also specific to our team. Do I acknowledge the presence of guilt—both self-imposed and the guilt that we can all lay on others—specific to our intentional mindset shifts around flexibility?

- Feeling a sense of belonging. Do I share my personal connection to the journey?

The concept of the Wise Engagement Meter accomplished several key goals for us. First, we wanted to encourage active involvement. Rather than simply measuring attitudes and other more abstract ideas, we wanted it to be hands-on and a call to action. In essence, we wanted every team member to consider what they were doing on that particular day to help build the Wise Firm. They could each make their choices and, from there, take steps to put those choices into practice. Team members could check in each day via their phones or on their computers.

To help strengthen the sense of shared mission, we also wanted to be sure that team members could know what others in the company were choosing on any given day to keep the push toward the Wise Firm moving forward. Using large television screens, we had a sort of ESPN-like scrolling menu that displayed team members' photos and their particular choice for that day. These screens were highly visible by design, placed in hallways, break rooms, meeting spaces, and other places where they could be readily seen by people as they went about their day. This was also scrolling on their computers when they logged into the company's intranet.

It was very different from just checking a box and responding to a survey question. The team members were charged with relating their goal for the day to some activity, task, or project. Not only did that help raise their ongoing awareness of the company's evolution, but they could also see what others were doing. That helped solidify the mindset of shared goals and coordinated teamwork. It was a constant reminder to everyone that we were building this together.

In fact, looking back on that, I'm not entirely sure that the term *engagement* really captured what we were trying to achieve. If we were doing it again, something like *magnetic energy* might be more appropriate. Whatever the name, it was a proactive tool that called people to action and, at the same time, served to strengthen their sense of mission and common cause. By identifying a particular vision and allowing people the discretion to choose what they wanted to do to help contribute progress toward that vision, that's where we knew we would get the extra oomph—the shared energy that built commitment, unity, and a determination to do whatever was necessary to reach our shared goal. The objective was to capture that discretionary effort as much as possible, that magnetic energy, that daily mindset of building something together.

A TRIP TO DISNEY

People have different primary motivators when they make the decision to commit to a cause or a team. For some, it's the alignment of their personal values, while others are primarily motivated by the purpose. We will find some people who are driven by the social aspects and a cause to give back in some way to others. For some, it's the mission or the big challenge that ignites their commitment. Of course, there are the people who are focused on the career aspects of the opportunity and they will want to know that they will be challenged and will learn something new before they make a commitment. Obviously, an organization needs to address the needs driven by each of these primary motivators. The magic happens when we can weave a compelling vision or story that brings them all together.

In a way, I liken it to what Walt Disney was able to achieve. With the overriding purpose to create happiness, Disneyland is always building, changing, and evolving. The essence of a Disney park and resort is an appeal to all the senses, and when they work together, well, you get that Disney magic.

This is the power of our story in building the Wise Firm together. Our compelling vision provided team members with the ability to connect to our community and tribe in ways that are meaningful to them. They bond in different ways—their personal values, their personal purpose, their personal faith, their personal dreams—to thrive with a sense of belonging that is so hard to find today. By building on a foundation of purpose, our team members provide that discretionary effort that generates magnetic energy that's similar to the magic that Disney has found to be so powerful. As we say at the Wise Firm, beBetter! God puts an innate desire in all of us to serve something bigger than ourselves. The Wise Firm embodied all the personal primary motivators that create high-performing teams.

In introducing the Wise Engagement Meter, we recognized that momentum would be essential to drive the vision that we had laid out for the company. We expected that, as buy-in from our team members increased and was noted and celebrated, we would have the force to continue to evolve and change in the way that we wanted to. Unknowingly, we stumbled onto a way to help measure our magnetic energy, the extra oomph everyone needs on their journey. And the Wise Engagement Meter allowed us to keep a beBetter mindset front and center every day.

Today, terms such as empowerment, engagement, and employee experience can be ubiquitous buzzwords. Every company on the block seems to be immersed in reinventing the ways overall company performance can be enhanced while implementing ideas to recruit and retain top-tier talent. As we learned back in 2013, just introducing new initiatives and programs isn't enough; you must measure your progress.

Admittedly, we had a long way to go. When we first started measuring engagement through the Wise Engagement Meter, our results were anything but encouraging. We were showing a dismal 19 percent engagement level. Not only was that eye opening in and of itself, but we also learned that it was very much in line with those of our counterparts. Real engagement wasn't merely a HORNE issue; it was symptomatic across our profession.

This was a brutal reality check for us—a company that had always spoken of its great culture. But, happily, it did offer some insight. First, we defined engagement as being when a team member personally made the choice and was inspired to give discretionary effort and focus, to be creative and embrace a beBetter mindset. And we began to realize that we would have to start measuring things that we had never even tried to measure before.

We overcame one obvious hurdle from the very beginning. High-performing teams are built on trust. Accordingly, we established from the outset that although we were measuring engagement as a team, we would never use people's lack of self-reporting against them. We were not about to confront someone and demand to know why they hadn't used the engagement meter in the past several days. The idea was to encourage and recognize active and involved participation, not to punish those who, for whatever reason, were less engaged.

We also made it clear that we would reward people for active participation in the Wise Engagement Meter. An offshoot of that approach came about six years later, when we introduced Wisely to replace the Wise Engagement Meter. This empowered our team members to reward each other for living the Wise Firm way. That turned out to be yet another effective method of not merely involving people but also keeping the Wise Firm journey foremost in people's minds as much as possible and providing real rewards for the behaviors, attitudes, and effort we wanted to retain.

It began to pay off over time. As the Wise Engagement Meter became an aspect of daily life at the firm, our numbers started to improve as trust began to grow. Having started at 19 percent, it only took us one year to boost that into the mid-30s, which then edged up toward the high 30s in year number two. We reached our most consistently high point at roughly 42 percent—more than twice the level of engagement from when we first started.

Even better, we knew that this tool set a rather high bar—measuring the will of people to take discretionary effort to share their mindset for the day (the power of magnetic energy once again). That kind of momentum proved essential further on, when we continued to introduce other measures to further our overall effort to build the Wise Firm.

"THE ENERGY TO PUSH THROUGH"

"When the firm first rolled out the Wise Engagement Meter, I was very skeptical. In fact, I did not participate the first six months or so. Then other team members asked me if I was on the meter or what was my Wise Firm mindset today. So I began to occasionally post on the meter. Overnight, I began to post every day, because I discovered something unique. When I selected my Wise Firm mindset for the day, it actually helped me stay focused on the most important thing I had that day. When I was having a bad day, it actually gave me the energy to push through it."

—Insights from HORNE team member blog

The Wise Engagement Meter also proved invaluable in identifying certain issues within the firm as it existed then. As time went on and we continued to gather data, our attention began to fix on several different metrics, one of which was employee turnover. We began to realize that lack of engagement—as measured via the Wise Engagement Meter—was one of the most reliable predictors of voluntary employee turnover. Although that seems rather obvious in retrospect, at the time, it was something of a revelation. We knew for the first time just what was contributing to the problem of excessive turnover.

But it was not at all surprising that, as the engagement numbers improved, our employee turnover decreased! On one level, we like to think that the effect of the engagement meter to promote inclusivity and to rally around a common mission played a role in that, but there were many overlaying factors that, over time, contributed to greater employee satisfaction and fulfillment. The meter did help us to recognize that we would do well to begin measuring other components of working at

HORNE—trust levels, connection to core values, and ability to reach their dreams, among others.

Those data points wouldn't merely measure change. They could help piece together the first steps toward putting the old HORNE out of business for good.

TRANSPARENCY AND "A GREAT PLACE TO WORK"

When starting out on a journey to totally recast anything—a group, an organization, a country—you have to expect that not everyone is going to be thoroughly comfortable with every step along that journey. And with regard to the genesis of the Wise Firm, one essential element that made a few people squirm in their seats had to do with transparency.

When we gathered data and insights on the company, we were committed to sharing that research with everyone in the firm. For instance, when we began to compile information regarding turnover, we made sure that data was available to anyone in the firm who wanted to review it. We went even further by sharing specifics—a breakdown of male versus female turnover, turnover of people of color, and the status of both gender and people of color leadership pipelines, to cite just a few.

It represented a significant pivot in terms of transparency. We wanted to have all our cards on the table so everyone would know where we were starting from and where we were headed. It was all about leadership accountability.

Moreover, it was a pivot that has remained in place. Year after year, we would share information, detail how we were acting on it, and then come back the following year to share the results of our efforts. We could pinpoint success as well as areas where we were still lacking. It represented a lasting commitment to ongoing transparency. It fostered our beBetter mindset in every way.

As I mentioned, not everyone in the company thought this was the best idea ever. For some, sharing proprietary information, warts and all, could prove a fine line to walk. They wondered what we stood to gain by doing it. Again, this was another defining moment; our board of directors did not blink. They held true to the long-term benefits of increasing trust with transparency. We were determined not to pretend that everything was functioning smoothly when, in fact, we all knew we had challenges and deficits that needed real attention. As it turned out, we left that approach to others.

I feel compelled to tell you that this level of transparency had some unintended consequences. In one of those early years, we took part in one of the abundant surveys from one of the "great place to work" vendors. We wanted to see where we stood in areas these types of surveys assessed—culture, advancement, communication, trust—in the eyes of our employees. The survey showed, among other things, that our team was highly concerned with our rate of turnover, a challenge our leadership had very openly talked about to the team. What made that interesting is, for some reason, many of the companies that ranked higher than ours in terms of great places to work had turnover similar to or higher than ours, but their own employees didn't see it as a problem. The difference? They weren't telling their employees it was a problem.

It was genuinely eye opening. We were obviously one of the few firms to openly acknowledge to our team members that turnover was an issue. And even though other companies may have avoided being transparent about turnover, everyone, including us, knew better. Most of the firms were just like us: turnover was an issue, whether they addressed it or not. In effect, lots of others were hiding a reality that we openly acknowledged. Everyone saw the truth. We chose to be transparent about our challenges, our hurdles—everything.

It proved to be a line in the sand for us. Moving forward, we agreed that being included on a "best places to work" list might be a nice recognition, but it would not provide momentum to really change our culture from good to great. Our goal was never to claim that everyone at HORNE— without exception—said they absolutely loved working here and that they couldn't find a single fault. Our goal was to have a strong sense of belonging so that we constantly worked to beBetter together.

FLEXIBILITY AND COVID-19

Although our commitment to fearless, unrivaled flexibility was invaluable to the growth of HORNE in and of itself, none of us could anticipate its role in helping us navigate one of the greatest challenges the company—and, for that matter, the entire world—confronted in recent years: the COVID-19 pandemic.

As businesses, schools, government offices, and most everything else began to go into lockdown in March 2020, we moved quickly to adjust our environment. First and foremost, we would offer as much safety as possible for every one of our teammates. At the same time, we also looked to maintain our professional activities at their highest level possible. We sent initial communications emphasizing that our teammates should take care of their families first and foremost; we would work together as we moved forward. With fearless, unrivaled flexibility already in full implementation, our team members were prepared to handle this new crisis.

Our champion of communication, Kassi Rushing, was ahead of the game as she prepared us with a communication strategy focused on the needs of our team members. People first was so evident in all of our plans.

Shortly into the pandemic, we were issuing best practices on a frequent basis to help our team members adjust to a new world with conflicting responsibilities and constant distractions. Coincidentally, we were able to share these best practices with our clients in 2020.

We also hosted frequent team meetings with myself and other leaders to continue to inform our team and provide them with access to our leadership. We also hosted Loop broadcasts, where team members could submit questions during the show, and we recorded these meetings so those who couldn't attend could listen later.

One of the incredible benefits of the pandemic, which also helps cultures thrive, is the flattening of organizations. More team members had access to and interacted with leaders during the pandemic. This expectation is here to stay, and magnetic cultures will use their technology, software, and leaders to connect, inform, and influence their teams.

A WORLD IN FLUX "MADE MORE STABLE"

More evidence that HORNE teammates supported our efforts at safety balanced with continued commitment to client care came by way of thank you notes to management, such as this one:

"I will say that with HORNE focusing on the safety of their people and serving our clients, it has made the spinning world seem more stable."

And another from a far-flung team member:

"HORNE of course has allowed me to truly work remotely, which is here in Edmonton, Alberta, Canada, so that I can be with my family at this extremely difficult time, and it means the world to me. Not sure what is going to happen to them both, but I am eternally indebted because while I am here supporting them, HORNE is here supporting me.

"I truly just want to say thank you. Thrilled to part of HORNE and have a sense of belonging!"

—*Insights from HORNE team member blog*

Although it was an understandably trying and frightening time for many, our established commitment to flexibility allowed us to adjust to the situation far more effectively than many of our counterparts. For one thing, as organizations and companies scrambled to institute more flexible and adaptive work arrangements, we were already well ensconced in that mindset. We were much more experienced in overseeing and managing fluid work arrangements. We could leverage communication and support better because those systems were already in place.

Just as important, our attitude toward flexibility made the shifts driven by COVID that much more comfortable. Everyone at HORNE was already familiar with the principle that it didn't matter how things were done so long as the results were positive. Our teammates knew what was expected of them, and they delivered accordingly. As others fretted over the uncertainty of work performed in unconventional settings and arrangements, we were much more confident in our teammates' commitment to accountability. We had already cleared that hurdle some time ago.

So, again by coincidence, God had us prepared with a strong culture and flexibility that made us distinctive and prepared to serve clients at a time they needed us most.

MAGNETIC THOUGHTS

"And we know that in all things God works for good of those who love Him, who have been called according to His purpose."

—ROMANS 8:28 NIV

"And God is able to bless you abundantly, so that in all things at all times, having all that you need, you will abound in every good work."

—2 CORINTHIANS 9:8 NIV

- To reach our goal to beBetter, we set a goal of fearless, unrivaled flexibility. We emphasized empowerment, autonomy, and freedom of choice. True flexibility would be unique for each team and individual team member.

- People are naturally more engaged if they feel they have real input into decision-making. The more avenues available for such participation, the greater the atmosphere of inclusion.

- Measurement matters—but make sure you measure the right things, not necessarily the easy ones. Start with measuring progress with your team's input. Be creative and explore what else will make a difference and then design methods for gathering it.

- We knew people would have to learn the discipline and responsibility that come with freedom. The more freedom we have, the more responsibility we have.

- Guilt vampires are real. We all have them. We get rid of them by talking about them, shining a light on them.

- Defining flexibility and providing individual choices are critical to meeting the expectations of your best talent; it's the freedom to make choices on when, where, and how we work.

- Flexibility does not mean less accountability. In fact, it boosts accountability, because more eyes are measuring results. The why behind one person's need for flexibility doesn't matter, but results and communication do.

- In introducing the Wise Engagement Meter, we recognized that momentum would be essential to drive the vision that we had laid out for the company; we went from 19 to 42 percent of employees feeling engaged at work—quite an improvement!

- Great leadership requires transparency across the organization, which includes posting our successes, as well as where we are still falling short.

- Culture change happens one conversation at a time. Every voice counts.

5

A Sense of Belonging

MANY OF US—PARTICULARLY BABY boomers—have bittersweet memories of going to homecoming dances during our high school days: the excitement of getting dressed up, of arriving at gymnasiums transformed with balloons and colored lights, the pound of a live band (or if you're a bit younger than me, a really good DJ) pumping out music that just made you want to move. But, then, just standing by all evening, alone along the sidelines—never being asked to dance or working up the courage to approach someone else. Then, the letdown of returning home and realizing it wasn't all you thought it was going to be.

As the momentum for transforming HORNE into the Wise Firm continued to build, it was this image of not dancing at a dance that I began to associate with this seminal issue of belonging. It became utterly apparent to me after chatting with a professor at a historically Black college. He spoke with pride of his son graduating from college and passing the CPA exam and, from there, going on to earn a position at one of accounting's Big Four firms.

His son described it as getting excited about being invited to the biggest dance in town, outfitting yourself in your best suit, but eventually realizing no one was really asking you to dance. As his father went on to explain, his son made numerous casual friends outside of the office, but it was completely different in the workplace itself.

He could feel a disconnect in team meetings with management, almost like his friends were creating a little distance between them. This was certainly a less inclusive feeling, where they avoided close interactions with him when management was around. He felt as though they were being cautious about their career by not engaging with him personally. Management, although very professional and nice, really made no attempts to know or connect with him in the same ways he saw they were with some of his White team members. There was lots of well-meaning talk, but not one step taken on the dance floor itself.

The story struck a chord in my heart. The bottom line was we all knew that diversity was simply a number, a measurement that means nothing on its own. Inclusion is only a game if people don't have a strong sense of belonging. Being included in the group is not the same as belonging.

A sense of belonging begins with each individual and requires extending trust, which must be matched by a leadership team that demonstrates they care. A sense of belonging actually fuels real inclusion, which is beyond simply being in the room. It's being in the room as yourself and feeling safe to be who you are. This safe place starts with leadership demonstrating trust and caring for people. By believing, trusting, and recognizing the good in people, connections grow and communities connect. It becomes magnetic as individuals are vulnerable and extend trust to each other.

Too many organizations, including the Big Four and other national firms, had very visible, well-intentioned initiatives for decades. Yet the progress within our profession was barely measurable—including at HORNE. This missed opportunity by companies is even more prevalent in the attrition that businesses are experiencing today as we share our story. McKinsey & Company stated on their blog and determined from their research with employees:

> *More than half of employees who left their job in the past*
> *six months did not feel valued by their organization (54*

percent) or manager (52 percent), or they lacked a sense of belonging (51 percent). Additionally, 46 percent cited the desire to work with people who trust and care for each other as another reason to quit. Employees want stronger relationships, a sense of connection, and to be seen.[7]

A sense of belonging is critical to magnetic culture and high performance. As we faced the brutal reality of our lack of belonging across our firm, I wasn't the only one who began to identify that pervasive feeling sadly similar to that memory of our youth—of people being left out, of groups excluded from something that they very much wanted to belong to.

In effect, we were beginning to realize that we had to move past the invitation and make a point of asking more people to actually dance. We needed to help each other find a true sense of belonging at the individual level that was both comprehensive and real. We had to demonstrate people before profits. We had to demonstrate we care about people and extend trust to each individual team member.

Trust and being vulnerable allow belonging to grow. People are searching to be part of something bigger than themselves. Each of us wants to know that our life and work have purpose. We knew this was about having significance in people's lives beyond success and financial rewards.

Belonging and trust come before high performance. A sense of belonging, the high-energy trust, is what makes a team a team. It's the cement and fuel for high-performing teams. It's this sense of belonging that transforms inclusion from an invitation to collaboration, commitment, and creativity. Let's say a full dance card! Only then can inclusion release the power of diversity.

It also reinforced the essential importance of the best culture possible.

---

7   Matt Fenton, Neel Gandhi, and Taylor Lauricella, "When the Grass Is Truly Greener: How Companies Are Retaining Frontline Talent," McKinsey.com (blog), January 31, 2022, https://www.mckinsey.com/business-functions/people-and-organizational-performance/our-insights/the-organization-blog/when-the-grass-is-truly-greener-how-companies-are-retaining-frontline-talent.

It became clear no program for diversity or inclusion could ever work if the culture wasn't there to support it. It wasn't enough to expand our recruiting pool. It wasn't enough to hire a more diverse group of teammates. Lacking a great culture, not even the best-intentioned initiative could prove successful or meaningful.

That was the genesis of our focus on Belonging at HORNE, which proved to be a singular confluence of powerful factors we knew we needed to leverage to help drive our culture's journey from good to magnetic.

A MAGNETIC MOMENT

In one of our early leadership summits where we invited virtually the entire firm, our featured speaker was Brian Biro. Brian is full of energy and focuses on the WOO that we each have. WOO stands for *window of opportunity*. Given that we had been emphasizing what a special time it was for us all, WOO seemed such an appropriate term. With WOO, we could build a magnetic culture, and we could beBetter. We were chasing greatness as a team.

Brian closed his presentation with an exercise that, to my mind, was one of the most connecting and magnetic moments of our entire journey. The energy that came from this summit and from this specific moment was like jet fuel for our team.

Brian set us up to each break a board with our arm, to break through to our future. On the side facing us, we all wrote the obstacle that was holding us back; on the other side, we wrote what opportunity or benefit we could have if we broke through this obstacle. This was life changing for many team members. Tears were shed, and people moved past barriers that had held them in fear.

As we closed this session, everyone had broken their board but Danny Meyers. Danny is a high-functioning quadriplegic team member who has decreased ability in his triceps. Despite those being the very muscles he needed to achieve this exercise, Danny was determined. He has more courage than I could ever dream of mustering. He rarely misses a day at work in our Ridgeland, Mississippi, office.

Brian went over and held Danny's board for him as about 100 of our team members gathered around.

Danny struck the board—nothing.

You could hear a gasp. Now about half the team was surrounding Danny's wheelchair.

Brian leaned in, and Danny struck again—nothing!

You could hear another gasp from the team. As Danny got ready to strike the board again, everyone—literally 400 or more people—circled around him, cheering him on.

Danny struck the board again—nothing. Now his arm was red, obviously stinging. We all started to move away, praising Danny for his courage.

"No, I want to do this," Danny announced. Our noisy conference room went completely silent.

"Danny, you can do this," Brian told him in a low voice. "Think and see your arm going right past the board."

The team rallied, cheering Danny every second.

Danny raised his arm, looked directly at the board, and struck it, and the board snapped like a firecracker.

People were crying everywhere. Seeing Danny smile, I doubt there was a person in that room who wasn't a mass of goose bumps. The sheer magnetic energy in the room was beyond anything I have experienced at any work event. People were cheering and chanting for the Wise Firm. Danny had broken through for all of us.

Lead by example. Every voice counts.

AN ORIGINAL BUILDING BLOCK

A sense of belonging was by no means a completely new, unnoticed objective. We had identified a feeling of inclusion as a critical component of the overall Wise Firm when we took our first transformative steps back in 2011.

But thanks to input from beBetter teams, as well as other avenues of our internal research, we began to realize just how much work we had to do when it came to building a genuine sense of belonging at HORNE. In particular, that came to an evident head in 2013, when we conducted a personal experience survey covering the entire company.

Turnover was a red flag. In 2013 alone, the firm had experienced the departure of 113 team members—nearly one-quarter of the entire company at the time. Of that total, 96 people were either female or people of color—a particularly disturbing finding. The total cost to HORNE was some $3 million by the most conservative calculations. And we couldn't even begin to put a number on the qualitative impact—the lost knowledge, the negative effect on client service, and the morale issues for the team left behind, to name just a few.

Our research confirmed many of the drivers for the voluntary turnover. Whether career navigation, support sources, access to leaders, equitable sponsors, adequate role models, or other factors, women and people of color were consistently reporting that there were effectively two HORNEs: one for them and another for everyone else.

However, it wasn't just a matter of demographics driving inequality. When we asked all team members to describe their experience at HORNE, we identified other factors that dictated the quality of team member experience. People were having vastly different experiences depending on their generation and age, which particular office they worked in, what team they belonged to, and who their leadership was.

The summation of that data and the key findings showed HORNE had a very consistent trend of inconsistent experiences. It brought home a reality we knew we could not ignore—that the goal of building the Wise Firm would be virtually impossible if only pockets of people experienced the vision.

But that recognition also presented us with a remarkable opportunity, and not just in boosting the sense of belonging for everyone who worked at HORNE. Nowhere in our journey of transforming our good culture into a high-performing great culture did the paths of God, faith, and culture intersect more than in our promise to have a strong sense of belonging.

Further than that, it was about building a culture based on love—genuine respect and care for others within the firm. Nothing could be more powerful in crafting an environment of true inclusion for all. As our friend John O'Leary always shares, "I love you, and there's nothing you can do about it."

But, without that, the dynamics and mindsets we wanted to instill in our people—to take the risks necessary to achieve high performance, to be better, and to truly care about others—would lack a meaningful foundation. It would simply be more window dressing.

ONE TEAM, ONE DIRECTION

"I appreciate HORNE's very real commitment to creating an amazing culture, what we call the Wise Firm. And part of our culture is to create a sense of belonging for each and every team member, where we embrace our differences and work in cohesion . . . living life together, one team, one direction. I can honestly say that HORNE wants every team member to have a sense of belonging. But as in any group, it can be challenging.

"There are definitely meetings when I am the only Black female in the room. I personally have struggled with speaking up most times. But does this mean I don't belong? I don't think so. When I feel out of place, I remember belonging means embracing our differences and accentuating each other's strengths. I see my team doing this, and we all have fun working together. I know I'm different, but what does that really mean?

continued

"We all are different in some way. Making the effort to get to know each other on an individual level and meet each other where we are is the goal. You see, the beauty of our Wise Firm culture is that it gives us the opportunity to define what Belonging at HORNE means to us individually. My advice on belonging: Make it personal. Every day you go to work, ask yourself, *What can I do to create a sense of belonging for myself and others?* It will change your perspective as you become intentional about breathing life into this part of our culture. Believe that, as different as we all are, each one of us is at HORNE for a reason. And while we're here, we must work together to build the Wise Firm. When we do that, we will truly believe the statement 'I belong at HORNE.'"

—Insights from HORNE team member blog

While a sense of belonging was an original building block of the Wise Firm, it wasn't until a few years later that we did the work of articulating six primary benefits of creating a culture that consistently emphasized inclusion:

- A sustainable growth model. A long-term approach to growing the company based on a strong, pervasive sense of belonging that would inevitably be distinctive among our clients.

- Sustainable succession. The greater the sense of inclusion, the stronger the succession pipelines. The leadership gap closes as the pipeline swells.

- Viable exit strategies. Constructive means of navigating teammate departures.

- Addressing talent shortages. Among other targets, a sense of belonging would bolster the firm's recruiting efforts at the college level.

- Greater diversity. The broader our base of teammates, the greater the range of expertise, skills, experience, and input. And that meant more innovation, improved creativity, and better outcomes for teams and clients.

- Improved overall performance. When people have a strong sense of belonging and feel secure where they are, it drives high performance for both the individual and the firm.

But again, there were critical advantages that reached far beyond the practical effects. Belonging at HORNE was built on the foundational faith and belief that we are all called by God to a higher purpose than ourselves, including to love and serve others. When we serve others, we believe that we are happier, more connected, and more energized.

Furthermore, it was a recognition that people will not care about your business or your clients until they know you care about them as individuals and see that, as an organization, we really are striving to help them reach their full potential. What makes us all better, what makes us all stronger, is what makes the individual better as well. There's no greater place than a sense of belonging where you find the convergence of God, faith, and culture.

NO STAND-ALONE INITIATIVE AND NO SILOS

As we had already identified a sense of belonging as one of the essential building blocks in constructing the Wise Firm, we recognized early on that this could not be an autonomous, focused campaign isolating one particular dimension of diversity or problem. Phrased another way, this wasn't just another stand-alone initiative. It was much more than that.

A sense of belonging was very much at the heart of everything involved in building the Wise Firm. We saw belonging as intentionally working together to create a culture where every team member could prosper and had the opportunity to reach his or her full potential. Belonging at HORNE, incorporating all diversity and inclusion objectives, was at the very foundation of the company's global developmental strategy for its people—each and every one.

While we wanted every member to feel like they were a part of the team, at the same time, Belonging at HORNE was not about merely fitting in. It was about the freedom and courage to be you. To be able to use your unique and individual strengths to serve in the ways that help you, your team, and the firm reach their full potential. It included the responsibility for each of us to help others grow their sense of belonging by being vulnerable, extending trust, and caring. This always starts with leadership.

Emily Parrish Miller, now a partner, had as much individual impact as any leader in our firm. She was and is an absolute role model for creating a sense of belonging by demonstrating the willingness to trust first, to care about people, to provide clarity on roles, to respect others, to express genuine kindness, to live through authentic leadership, and to support everyone on her team. Early in her career, Emily worked in several focus areas, and on each opportunity, the teams were left stronger and more united due to her influence. With her ability to grow teams with a strong sense of belonging, she became a role model for us and paved her way to partnership. Emily demonstrated for all of us the importance of extending trust, encouraging, respecting, showing appreciation, and connecting to team members. She is a champion in our quest for a strong sense of belonging.

That sort of language was not being used at all at that time. So, once again, we were outliers in our industry. But we understood that the secret sauce for high-performing teams was a concrete, meaningful sense of belonging—not just another feel-good, largely cosmetic campaign directed at specific elements of the company. A sense of belonging needed to be imbued in everything we said and did, which is how it went well beyond the purview of a limited initiative. It was going to impact everything, and we knew it from the very beginning.

Furthermore, we wanted to be certain that the effort was truly inclusive of everyone at HORNE. We intentionally chose a path where we kept everyone together. By that, we consciously avoided the sort of siloed approach that some other companies were pursuing—measures geared only to women, for instance, or people of color, even though almost every best practice we encountered at the time told us we would fail if we did not delineate our target more. But, as we saw it, creating silos would only serve to separate us more than bring us together.

To be clear, we did put practical strategies in place to address the needs of and to close gaps within specific team members—more on that later—but always within the larger context of a sense of belonging. It was a different approach than some wanted, but the most popular initiatives executed in the traditional ways in other companies weren't driving real change. We instinctively knew we had to pull together, and we needed our team members helping to solve these critical issues. In 2016, *Harvard Business Review* issued the results of a study on why companies were failing to make significant progress with diversity, which supported our observations on the lack of effectiveness of so many traditional diversity programs. The research included many best practices that we had already implemented.[8]

And, as our team members' own stories exposed, the effort to create a true sense of personal belonging applied to many broader cultural contexts, including where they happened to grow up.

A CHEESEHEAD COMES TO HORNE

"My story begins in Green Bay, Wisconsin, where I was born and raised. I then moved to Mississippi when I was 24 to attend graduate school. I did this because I believed (and still do, as much as ever) that we grow the most when we step out of our comfort zone.

"As a bit of a cultural transplant, during my first year at HORNE, I spent a lot of time assessing and acclimatizing. During that time, my performance advisor helped me realize that maybe

continued

---

8   Frank Dobbin and Alexandra Kalev, "Why Diversity Programs Fail," *Harvard Business Review*, July–August 2016, https://hbr.org/2016/07/why-diversity-programs-fail.

I wasn't being vulnerable enough to build a sense of connection or fully experience the present.

"In order to change that, I decided I needed to build better relationships with my team members. I have found that many of the conversations that have developed my sense of belonging have not been about work. For example, when our firm held an event at the Dallas Cowboys' stadium, I wore my Green Bay Packers cheesehead and met a team member who had also lived in Green Bay for a period. Every year at HORNE's annual Summer of Service, I've been able to build a deeper and more meaningful connection with someone on my project team as we volunteer with an organization in our community. Each year, someone has taken the opportunity to share why the specific organization we are serving holds such a meaningful place in their heart. The more I saw others be vulnerable, the more comfortable I felt with being vulnerable.

"At HORNE, I feel like my team is uniquely invested in me. When I bought my first home, one of the partners on our team told me how important it was to him that I had time off to move in and get settled while my family visited from out of state (even if I was a day or two short on PTO). Months later, another partner shared that he had expressed at a partnership meeting that watching multiple team members settle in their first home had been a measure of success for him this year. I know these same leaders are invested in me enough to challenge me with tough feedback. I appreciate that we have an open and honest dialogue about my strengths and weaknesses. I know that I am ultimately in control of my own success, but I feel confident my team has given me the foundation and structured feedback that I need to reach my full potential."

—Insights from HORNE team member blog

We knew our goal was a strong sense of belonging for everyone. Loving, caring, respecting, forgiving, and celebrating each other was paramount in how we served each other. We were striving for unity, not uniformity. For us, that made a different path the obvious choice, one where we created platforms and vehicles where everybody got to, as I like to say, help pull the rope.

DUAL RESPONSIBILITY

If Belonging at HORNE was to take hold and produce the critical results we were looking to achieve, one overriding reality was the essential involvement of everyone at HORNE—that everyone who believed in the message and mindset we were advocating would lend a hand in pulling the rope.

That led to a few challenges. As was the case with other strategies we were developing and implementing to reinvent HORNE, we didn't naively expect everyone working for the company at the time to be completely on board with what amounted to a core shift in how we did everything.

Traditionally, businesses employ a common sequence of priorities—first growth, next customers, with people taking up the rear. We began our journey by flipping those priorities completely on their head—first came people who, in turn, compose the Wise Firm, customers came second, and growth was number three. Our philosophy was, if we built the optimal culture and our subsequent focus was on our clients' success, growth would naturally come. The numbers would always show up in big ways when we got culture right.

Although others outside of HORNE have also seen the wisdom of focusing on people first rather than growth (noted author and consultant Patrick Lencioni refers to numbers as an issue where too many organizations expend far too much energy), there were some within HORNE who didn't quite share that viewpoint. Although we didn't agree or reach a consensus, we did agree to move forward together with a focus on our people. This resulted in our strategic planning starting with culture and people as the top priority each year. Then we discussed services and clients. Finally, we began to put expectations for growth and numbers based on our commitments to the first two priorities.

During that time, we often focused on a central question: Does everyone belong at HORNE? And we had to be okay with saying no. We just knew it made sense to recognize the reality that not everyone's going to believe or align with our core values and who we were aspiring to be. But our core values mattered, and we had to honor those above anything else.

For some, all this sounded as though we were talking out of both sides of our mouth. On one hand, they felt we were championing individual autonomy and responsibility, and, in the same breath, we were pointing out that people had a choice to either get on board or look for a more suitable setting elsewhere—our way or the highway.

But for those of us who were, in fact, committed and aligned, we wanted and actually cared that each person at HORNE had a strong sense of belonging. Furthermore, we also knew that everyone would not choose to belong at HORNE. And that was perfectly okay. We wanted people to be fully vested in whatever they truly believed in. And, in emphasizing that it was acceptable not to buy in, we were also making it clear that comprehensive acceptance and support were central to our effort.

Moreover, to be perfectly forthright on another matter, when we talked about belief, that didn't refer to a belief in God or adherence to any particular religion or faith. Rather, belief meant a recognition of the importance of service to others. By belief, we emphasized caring about one another, the importance of progress for the group rather than the individual, respect for all team members, and, finally, a commitment to pursuing your highest and best use. Belief was as much a matter of attitude as it was faith.

To be clear, although our first core value references God and honoring personal faith, belief in God is not a requirement to be a team member. We honor a person's personal faith even if they are atheists, and we welcome nonbelievers on the team. The buy-in is about service to others, family, and gratitude. On the other hand, we celebrate that, for those who believe in God, our service honors Him.

That led to an emphasis on two primary engagement points, both of which addressed a form of responsibility. One was organizational responsibility—what the company's obligation was to craft a workplace where people were in an optimal position to achieve their full potential. This meant trust had to be built, and that starts with leadership being vulnerable and extending trust to team members. Additionally, there was the importance of team member responsibility—what each individual could contribute in a consistent, ongoing basis to help build trust and a workplace with consistent values.

This wasn't about imposing rules—what either the firm or an individual "had" to do to contribute. (As anyone who knows me will tell you, I dislike rules. They're way too easy to hide behind.) Rather, this was about a true feeling of teamwork—a strong sense of responsibility rather than a mandate.

In so doing, we helped establish a collaborative, accountable relationship, one in which both the company and the individual played a central role in helping to build a sense of belonging, a lynchpin of the Wise Firm.

WHAT ABOUT ME?

Among other challenges, one of the earliest obstacles we faced with Belonging at HORNE was where to focus our efforts first. We knew that we wanted every team member to feel a strong sense of belonging company-wide, but we also recognized that there were certainly particularly problematic areas that warranted more immediate consideration.

Employing a risk model derived from extensive data collection, women and people of color were two groups identified as high risk. By that, I mean we knew those two groups would need particular forms of support, advocacy, and other methods to help cement their feeling of genuinely belonging at HORNE.

Our data supported that conclusion. For instance, women were not being promoted at the same rate as their male colleagues. Moreover, it was an issue that many people noticed, not necessarily just those directly affected. In one particular employee survey, almost three-quarters of the respondents said that the company needed to abandon career assumptions based on gender. That reflected an overall problem of making decisions for people without actually understanding their own dreams for their career. In effect, we were making choices impacting others without knowing whether it was truly in their best interests or even always understanding what the impact was.

However well intentioned our thinking was, we also understood that our desire to target groups with particularly problematic issues could be misconstrued. Put simply: What about me? If you weren't necessarily a member of a group identified as high risk, what was your source of support? Just because you didn't happen to be female or a person of color, that didn't necessarily mean your feeling of belonging at HORNE was absolute. If you needed help to boost your sense of inclusion, would that take a back seat to others whose need was, statistically speaking, greater than yours?

Fortunately, we had several factors working in our favor. For one thing, we had extensive research to support our conclusions. The numbers simply didn't lie when it came to documenting pockets within the company that mandated particular attention and effort. The numbers painted a glaring disparity for everyone to see: Starting with our turnover percentages in 2012 to 2014, we were seeing 5 to 10 percent more for our women and people of color team members than in our overall firm. Our promotions to manager and senior manager for the same three years demonstrated lower rates of promotions for women and people of color. The percentage of women in our partner group was less than 20 percent, and we had no partners who were people of color.

Our experience survey revealed many reasons or behaviors that contributed to our women and people of color team members having inconsistent or even bad experiences. Women and people of color agreed less or disagreed more with the following statements about their personal experience:

- I understand how to increase my contribution to the firm.

- I understand how to advance in my career.

- Everyone can advance within the firm, regardless of gender, race, color, religion, ethnicity, or age.

- The firm's efforts to retain and develop talent have helped me personally to identify potential barriers to my success.

- I have increased my leadership responsibilities within the firm or within my client engagements during the past year.

- I feel a sense of belonging or fit with the HORNE team.

- I feel there is someone in the firm who has my long-term career interests in mind and works on my behalf to ensure I have the proper assignments to continue my advancement.

- I feel there is someone in the firm who understands my vision for my career and life and is there as a mentor or coach to assist me when I am challenged with this vision.

Overall, we analyzed our team members' work experiences from the lenses of geography, age, gender, and race. The greatest gaps in experience were expressed by our women and people of color team members who identified access, inclusion, and fit as their number-one barrier.

We boldly shared the data that demonstrated differences in experiences. This data—communicated transparently and often—helped us overcome intense and complex emotions for providing an equitable playing field for everyone. These ongoing measurements gave us a solid framework for moving forward.

Another major advantage was our determination not to subdivide the overall effort into silos where we would effectively separate groups for different forms of programs and effort. By continually emphasizing throughout that this was a company-wide effort effectively targeting everyone—albeit with certain priorities in place—we were able to convey a sense of unity and of moving forward as a group, the exact sort of environment we were looking to strengthen through the Belonging at HORNE program. We wanted to be as transparent as possible with our intentions, as well as the reasoning and data behind what we did.

We saw retention of women and people of color improve. We saw pipelines of talent diversify, ultimately yielding more partners who were women and people of color. In January 2022, we saw the promotion of five women and one man into the partnership. Our ownership group has grown from 0 to almost 6 percent people of color and is more than 30 percent women. These are some of the tangible results we had in mind when Belonging at HORNE was born.

An additional but no less critical factor in developing the Belonging at HORNE effort was our commitment to remain true to ourselves, to rely on what we ourselves knew to be the issues and the best ways of approaching them. The beauty of our progress is that we focused on everyone dancing and dancing to their own music. Only a true sense of belonging can get everyone on the dance floor.

When many companies start down a culture-building path, it can be far too tempting to defer to the ideas and opinions of outside experts—consultants who observe what is going on and then recommend a predefined course of action that they've generally used elsewhere. Although we did involve some outside consultants on our journey who offered wise counsel and advice, we remained truly committed to decisions and ideas that were consistent with who we ourselves knew we were as a company.

If we were to craft an organization where individualism and autonomy were central to our culture, it wouldn't come about with a somewhat prefabricated program whose primary selling point was that a lot of other companies had used the same principles. If our own issues were singular to our company, a cut-and-paste approach would likely prove a considerable waste of time, money, and energy.

It all came back to our particular understanding of HORNE—where we were and where we specifically wanted to go. It brought home the absolute necessity of doing the hard legwork of truly coming to know the specifics and wrinkles of your company and then figuring out particular ways that will prove effective for that particular group. We were leery of cookie-cutter, three-step plans to creating an environment of belonging just because it had been used elsewhere. It was critical to recognize that their challenges and opportunities would likely not be the same as ours.

THE KICKOFF—AND AN EPIPHANY

By this point in the overall Wise Firm journey, we had completed a number of critical steps. First, we had looked our brutal reality squarely in the eye. Where was everyone's sense of belonging at HORNE? With people throughout the company reporting different experiences and satisfaction levels, how could we rework the company's culture so that everyone felt a genuine sense of inclusion and opportunity?

We then took our findings and observations to the board of directors in 2013 to show them precisely where we were and what we intended to do to address issues we felt were central to the company's future. To their credit, the board enthusiastically embraced both the reality that we presented and the specific programs and strategies we recommended. We then took particular care to communicate with all our partners in small, personal meetings. We showed them the same data, explained the vision, answered their questions, and called them to action. We would need their leadership to bring this to life. Again, it was our partner group who championed and led us to a stronger sense of belonging.

Accordingly, to signal the kickoff of the overall commitment, we set aside a specific week to celebrate Belonging at HORNE. The week was filled with activities and events geared to letting everyone in the company understand exactly what we planned to do and how they could take part in this critical effort. It was both fun and focused. It was a commitment of time and expense, which paid off over and over again.

But it proved to be much more than a celebration. Through the work of our beBetter teams, as well as an exercise that everyone in the company took part in during that kickoff week, by sheer coincidence, we stumbled onto a paralyzing hidden challenge that was silently stalling our journey from good to great.

Basically, our stumbling block was this: We were too nice. We had created a false harmony within our firm due to conflict avoidance. This included team members who were simply afraid or untrusting enough to provide the candor, the feedback, the creative ideas, and overall collaboration to challenge the status quo and help us to beBetter.

First, let me back up just a bit. Throughout my extensive time at HORNE—as well as that of a countless number of my colleagues—HORNE had a reputation as a nice place to work. The company employed nice people who did nice work. All in all, nice seemed the optimal word to capture working at HORNE.

Following our Belonging at HORNE kickoff week, I had numerous meetings with various beBetter team members in small group settings, discussing what we had learned from the week itself, and to get their input on major challenges the company was confronting (as I always like to say, one conversation at a time). As the conversations evolved, a common theme began to appear repeatedly: conflict avoidance. As many team members told me, there was a pervasive and ongoing avoidance of any sort of healthy, constructive conflict. Many at HORNE routinely skirted the sorts of difficult conversations that every healthy organization needs to have, be they about performance, career advancement, or any number of central issues. We were being nice—to our own detriment.

As I came out of those meetings, I was taken aback. Looking back, we should have seen this on our own. It was so obvious and prevalent. It was a troubling revelation but, as it turned out, also an invaluable one. It became apparent that many HORNE teammates were not receiving the candid feedback they felt they needed. Just as apparent was how relevant that was to Belonging at HORNE. Until we could get a grasp on this widespread problem and begin building a culture that welcomed healthy, open conflict and consistent feedback from all team members, we would have a decidedly uphill struggle to address all the other issues that we wanted to take on. We were just not having the conversations we needed to have.

In fact, we eventually earmarked conflict avoidance as another massive hurdle to achieving a sense of belonging at HORNE. We clearly lacked the level of trust that we both wanted and needed. Moreover, our self-awareness was not sufficient to see that people were still at times holding back—a false harmony that impeded progress throughout the firm.

Additionally, we realized that the problem of conflict avoidance ran counter to so many of the principles that we were working to espouse. It wasn't forthright. It wasn't transparent. It didn't reflect the sense of caring that we promoted at HORNE. To care about and support our colleagues, we needed to be able to hold them accountable to their commitments, to help them recognize their own barriers. The most unloving, uncaring attitude we could take was to wordlessly tolerate underperformance from anyone, leadership included.

Conflict avoidance and false harmony are hidden cancers in most organizations that eat away at culture and trust every day. It is one of the barriers to high performance that's easiest to fool ourselves about. Certainly, conflict avoidance and an inability to have hard conversations aren't generally what emerge from organization-wide efforts to boost diversity and inclusion. But, happily, as we began to introduce the varied elements that would compose our Belonging at HORNE effort, that was what we identified as one of the core hurdles to be overcome. Moving forward, we made certain to address them at every possible opportunity.

Evidence of our success in creating a sense of belonging began to grow. According to a 2017 survey of HORNE teammates:

- 91 percent said HORNE was a great place to work.

- 82 percent felt they were making a difference at HORNE.

- 90 percent said they felt a strong sense of belonging.

- 82 percent believed they could achieve their dreams at HORNE (testimony to our effort to build our leadership pipeline, particularly for women and people of color).

MAGNETIC THOUGHTS

"Therefore, as God's chosen people, holy and dearly loved, clothe yourselves with compassion, kindness, humility, gentleness, and patience."

—COLOSSIANS 3:12 NIV

"Without love, there is no reason to know anyone, for love in the end will connect us to our neighbors, our children, and our hearts."

—MARTIN LUTHER KING JR.

- People won't truly embrace even the most beneficial objectives unless they have a true sense of belonging, and no program for diversity or inclusion could ever work if the culture wasn't there to support it.

- Understanding that some people can feel excluded isn't enough to address the issue. The cause for that sense of disconnection must be identified and addressed. Diversity is simply a number and inclusion is optics without a strong sense of belonging for each team member. Everyone needs to dance!

- Nowhere in our journey of transforming our good culture into a high-performing, great culture did the paths of God, faith, and culture intersect more than in our promise to have a strong sense of belonging. It starts with caring and extending trust to each other.

- Although feelings of exclusion or being an outsider are often attributed to a fairly predictable list of causes—such as specific demographics—other elements can come into play and often compound those feelings, including work location, life experiences, perceptions, quality of leadership, life phase, and local team assignment.

- Creating a people-first culture requires a focus on people and culture as a top priority in the strategic plan. Starting with this priority sends the right message to everyone and provides for a better allocation of resources.

- While we wanted every member to feel like they were a part of the team, at the same time, belonging is not about merely fitting in; it's about the freedom and courage to be you. It's about being able to use your unique and individual strengths to serve in ways to help everyone—you, your team, and the firm—reach full potential. A strong sense of belonging starts with leadership. Leadership must be first to trust, be vulnerable, and make the efforts to connect to team members.

- Finding the strategy that invites everyone to help pull the rope is critical for real growth and progress in our desire to build inclusion and unleash the power of diversity. Be intentional for all high-risk groups while helping everyone grow stronger from the process.

- Be aware of the conflict avoidance that permeates so many organizations. In our experience, being too nice got in the way of improvement. Avoiding the tough conversations wasn't forthright, it wasn't transparent, and it didn't reflect the sense of caring that we promoted at HORNE.

6

Love and Care

"LOVE IS RESPONSIBLE CARING FOR each team member. True love is not easy, no birds or bees, but is unselfishly concerned more about others than one's self." Those words, written by our late friend and colleague Charles Curry, wonderfully encapsulate one of the cornerstones of the Wise Firm—truly loving and caring for one another. Moreover, we stand for not just pockets of such an attitude but prioritizing loving and caring for one another throughout the entire firm—leadership, satellite offices, everyone. Lacking that, the Wise Firm certainly would not prove capable of all that it could potentially become.

How do we define loving and caring? Respect, appreciation, support, forgiving, and recognition, among other components. This means prioritizing others—as Charles so aptly put it—more so than we might prioritize ourselves. It was clear that such values were necessary to create the magnetic energy we sought—the force to move people to do things above and beyond with joy and commitment.

But it wasn't going to happen all by itself. One of the ongoing lessons we experienced throughout our journey to create the Wise Firm was the often downplayed but critical disparity between wonderful ideas and actual action. As we ourselves had seen throughout our industry, many programs designed to foster any number of benefits were put into place with the best of intentions—only to falter in an effort to execute them.

Put another way, we recognized that, to truly love and care for others, a sense of belonging must be put into action. In order to build a culture of belonging, we knew we needed pragmatic steps to push those noble ideals into being. It reminded me of a passage from the book of James: "Faith without works simply isn't real."

Early on, we had established our commitment to complete and utter transparency. That was an essential component to build an environment of true belonging. In particular, we knew that everyone at HORNE had to remain informed of all the changes and the overall reinvention that was taking place all around them. We also quickly learned that we would have to be explicit in explaining why certain actions were prioritized and others were not. Many times over, we found out that most people have a hard time connecting the dots for themselves, so we had to be direct, transparent, and detailed with much more repetition of our messages than some of us liked.

This commitment to both transparency and action began most visibly with the formation of our Belonging at HORNE task force, which would be charged with, among other issues, developing our action plans for increasing belonging and maintaining our commitment to transparency.

THE BELONGING TASK FORCE: TRANSPARENCY

Recognizing the value of a point group to spearhead the overall Belonging at HORNE journey, the board of directors moved quickly to assemble a special Belonging at HORNE task force to provide direction, priority of action, feedback, and insight. Initially composed primarily of partners, directors, and senior management, the committee was charged not only with championing the company's reinvention when it came to a sense of belonging, but also with assuming a high level of accountability to ensure everything that we wanted to happen did, in fact, happen. We recognized early on that this task force would become an essential means of listening to and responding to the needs of our team members. As a result, we would eventually merge other internal committees into this one, which allowed us to consistently emphasize that all people decisions would derive from a priority of belonging first and foremost.

One of the first and most unique steps that the initial Belonging task force took—in line with our commitment of transparency—was to ensure that the company published an internal annual report detailing the specific elements of our efforts. In so doing, we would offer comprehensive insight into various strategic priorities, as well as those goals that had been earmarked for that specific year. Over the years, the specifics of those reports have varied. In some years, we offered management's view of how we were making progress; in others, we highlighted how team members throughout the company were experiencing their jobs.

But no matter the particulars of a given year, the steering committees' annual reports have become a bedrock that embodies HORNE's lasting commitment to transparency and accountability. Given the significant resources we were committing to the overall effort, we recognized that if HORNE team members as a group weren't fully informed and supportive of those measures, any attempt at sweeping reinvention would almost surely fall short. Once again, we needed everyone on board to enact genuine change.

Every bit as important, the initial Belonging task force and all subsequent task forces have become one of our absolute best practices. For one thing, not only did they prove instrumental in the initial stages of Belonging at HORNE, but steering committees throughout the years have also been an important voice for our colleagues, serving as representatives of the varying dimensions of diversity within our employee base. We made efforts to boost the members' visibility and to encourage our team members to speak with any steering committee member when questions, ideas, or concerns arose.

In so doing, we avoided the problems that many companies make, however unintentionally. For instance, it has been a relatively common practice to designate a chief compliance officer or to funnel diversity and other critical issues to human resources. This is well intentioned but, more often than not, inadequate to achieve real change in areas that should receive the highest priority. Too often, the offices of diversity dissolve into issues of mere compliance, a check-the-box cosmetic obligation. We wanted more.

By contrast, by assembling committee members who represented belonging throughout the company, there's a much greater call to real action, not to mention broader viewpoints, feedback from different vantage points, and more accountability. In our experience, steering committees tackle real problems and set achievable priorities on issues with genuine impact.

Perhaps even more valuable, the Belonging task force quickly grew into an actionable forum for the issue of conflict avoidance that we all recognized we would have to confront sooner rather than later. Our goal was to embrace radical candor and healthy conflict to allow every voice to count while the power of diverse thinking helped us beBetter. The Belonging task force gatherings were anything but stereotypical business meetings—formal and dripping with protocol. Rather, they became a venue, a safe place for open, often difficult discussions—so challenging, in fact, that the committee members would leave meetings emotionally spent but also utterly energized by the candor and significance of the conversation.

In fact, more than a few tears were shed in the Belonging task force meetings as the members grew in their awareness of challenges, their own privilege, and opportunities. Sometimes, it was a matter of coming to truly understand a very real problem. Just as often, it was the realization of how much many of us were part of the problem itself. That made those meetings so much more than a list of cold, abstract agenda items. They were very heartfelt experiences, very much rooted in the beliefs and values that we all inevitably returned to, time and again.

In particular, two people need to be cited for making the Belonging task force the valuable and ongoing success that it is. First is the late Charles

Curry, who, at the time, was senior manager in government services in our Houston office. Charles was one of the first Belonging task force members and, as a person of color, was instrumental in addressing issues of race and other topics related to diversity.

But, true to the nature of the evolving Wise Firm, Charles never dealt with those sorts of sensitive topics caustically or with bitterness. Rather, in discussing the challenges faced by teammates who were people of color, he was inevitably compassionate, gentle, and focused on changing things for the better. His invaluable participation never once held an edge of acrimony.

Charles opened our eyes to so many things that we could do better. Perhaps even more important, he was so loving by nature, always tackling delicate questions with a safe place for others. He inevitably gave you the benefit of good intentions.

The tribute the company released upon Charles's passing summarized it perfectly:

> *Charles was a fearless leader. Not because he was never scared but because he found the courage to push through his own fear. He took on challenges that many of us have never known or had to deal with. His ability to give others the benefit of good intentions was powerful. He spoke with wisdom and insight, and when he spoke, we all certainly listened. He had a gift for delivering truth with gentleness, refusing to shy away from hard conversations, whether about accountability or belonging. He set an example for everyone at HORNE—everyone.*

A second Belonging task force member who warrants particular attention is managing partner of health care Kathy Watts. Kathy was appointed by the board of directors as the inaugural chairperson of the Belonging task force and served in that capacity for a number of years. But her involvement goes far beyond mere longevity. Having worked in a variety of settings in the company as the proverbial "only woman in the room,"

Kathy made certain that issues pertaining to women received every bit as much attention as any challenge facing the company. Much like Charles, she was adept and persuasive in conveying the viewpoint of a particular group of teammates, helping to expand the entire committee's understanding of the unique and often frustrating environment that many women in the company faced.

Both Charles and Kathy occupied positions that every great organization needs to fill—that of inspiring role models for others. Every great movement needs giants, catalysts driving change, and Charles and Kathy were and are two such champions.

Magnetic energy always grows more leaders who pick up the rope. Alethia Thomas is another such leader—our young champion who followed in the footsteps of Charles and Kathy in influencing our journey forward.

Ultimately, the Belonging task force was one of our first significant steps, not only because of the actions driven or accountability derived, but because it pushed us toward learning how to be comfortable with the uncomfortable. In fact, over time, many of us realized that we would never be completely comfortable with some of the issues facing us. But we saw that as an initial mark of success. We were becoming courageous enough to have the conversations that mattered—to be open to experiences that weren't necessarily our own—and trying to understand how they were contributing to pockets of differences within the firm.

SPONSORSHIP AND ADVOCACY

The work of the Belonging task force, as well as other initiatives, underscored a core component of the overall effort to build the Wise Firm—that a sense of belonging is everything and that no one achieves their full potential without feeling safe and supported. Their work also brought an awareness to the forefront that we all need sponsors and advocates who help us along the way. No one gets there on their own.

Accordingly, one of the first and most impactful actions of the steering committee was to introduce the concept of sponsorship to the firm—and to educate everyone at HORNE about what that entailed and the importance that it take place equitably. Then, we ultimately (and quickly) developed and introduced a formal sponsorship and advocacy program as part of our overall leadership development strategy.

This particular initiative was a two-year program and an important part of our formal leadership development programming. At its outset, it paired high-performing, high-risk team members with partners and senior leadership. The idea behind the concept of sponsorship was to bring together promising team members (high-performing) who had gaps in their experience, little visibility, or specific issues to address (high-risk) together with others who already had a proverbial seat at the table. In so doing, we wanted to offer a comprehensive, one-on-one structure in which rising team members could articulate their career goals and aspirations, as well as what challenges and obstacles they felt were standing in their way. They would then receive the support they needed through their sponsor to navigate the organization.

The program helped open the eyes of countless team members to what was truly possible to achieve—provided that they were open to accepting help and guidance from those who were willing to share. This resulted in stars being released toward their full potential, which, otherwise, might have dimmed or chosen to shine on another horizon. There are so many to share here, yet perhaps a couple of examples will trigger the vision of similar talent in your organization.

A female person of color team member who was very high potential participated in one of our earlier sponsorship groups. Although her team leaders thought very highly of her potential, she found herself struggling with the question of access, fit, and understanding how to advance her career. The sponsorship program opened her eyes to how the firm worked, grew her network of decision makers, and gave her confidence to be herself and to own her voice. She accelerated her growth and received numerous promotions, raises, and bonuses. She is a leader on some of our biggest projects today. She now participates as a sponsor for others.

Caring and giving back builds a stronger sense of belonging and becomes magnetic for other team members.

In another example, a female team member was really struggling with the belief that she could contribute at a high level and also be a mother. Her participation in the sponsorship program resulted in growing advocacy that she could choose appropriate boundaries and integrate her career with her family. She gained exposure to other partners who helped open doors for her to step into leadership. Her career advancement has soared; she is now a partner who is continuing to excel and grow.

The last one I will share was a female team member who was working on an almost completely male team. She felt like a fish out of water and was dealing with some strong personalities. The sponsorship program helped her access the support she needed to understand more of what she really wanted to do. This advocacy helped her own her voice in how she wanted to lead in this group. She actually wanted to lead an area that she was not working in when she started the sponsorship program.

Eventually, she made the recommendation to the team leaders, received the approval to change roles, and has been a growing leader for this team. This has resulted in other women not only being recruited and retained but moving into key roles to help with the exponential growth for this group. Magnetic!

INHERENT STRENGTHS

The program possessed a number of inherent strengths. For one thing, it helped bring together people who otherwise might never have had any sort of relationship at all—overcoming the perceived distance that many in organizations of all sorts might feel toward leadership. Moreover, the program often paired people who were simply very different from each other—in background, personality, and other characteristics. Once again, we looked to the opposite of what many other companies were doing— partnering people with similar backgrounds on the well-meaning but often mistaken assumption that they could "relate" better.

Additionally, we were very intentional in our use of the terms *sponsors* and *advocates* rather than the more common label of *mentors*. Mentors may offer advice and feedback—certainly valuable counsel but limited in ownership of the relationship. They certainly may have walked a path similar to the people they mentor, but their involvement can be constrained, either by design or choice.

Put simply, a sponsor has a good deal more skin in the game. They are a person who intentionally uses their political capital to help another person progress in the organization. Their name is genuinely attached to another person; that person's success reflects on the sponsor.

Naturally, sponsors offer suggestions and counsel, but their relationship goes far beyond a sounding board. First, accomplished leaders acting as sponsors can leverage their own capital and influence to help their protégé move forward and navigate the organization more effectively. In one respect, that could mean introducing sponsored teammates to others within the company who, in their own way, can help benefit career trajectories—allowing the protégé to become involved in significant projects—for example, simply coming to know someone with particular insights and ideas that can prove enormously helpful.

We also came to emphasize what we referred to as stretch assignments. For example, sponsors might suggest that their protégé be included in a certain project or some other responsibility that challenged their skills and capabilities. Even if it were a fairly modest reach, it nonetheless would serve to move a person's career forward by exposing them to new experiences, contacts, and activities.

Even as the managing partner, I chose to participate as a sponsor in our very first pilot program. It was eye opening, to say the least. Simply put, I was naive about how personal, connecting, and impactful this initiative would be, not only the protégé but also for the sponsor.

I was matched with Lynn Seals, a Black female senior manager in our government consulting services who joined the firm as an experienced hire. As we began our session to get to know each other, I was both excited and apprehensive. Lynn and I knew each other from a couple of years earlier when we worked together on a project.

In our sponsorship program, the first step is to connect by knowing each other much more intimately. As Lynn and I got to know each other on a personal basis, we found we had so many things in common. We laughed and shared family stories. I got to know and love her family. Lynn gave me a safe place to ask questions, to speak freely without worrying about making mistakes.

Somewhat after the fact, I also came to know that Lynn was initially skeptical about the sponsorship effort. She thought it was essentially an exercise in entitlement—just another feel-good program with little in the way of widespread, meaningful impact.

But Lynn's participation in the program changed her mind. She began to provide me insights into her perspective and the overall perspective of our Black and African American team members. Her stories about some of their experiences rocked my confidence that we could truly be a firm with a strong sense of belonging for everyone. We had so far to go; so much of the iceberg was under the water.

Lynn has since retired from our firm, but she left us stronger and better in so many ways. Lynn is the type of champion that a culture must have to beBetter. Her thoughts on the experience reflect my own:

"You have been a sponsor advocating for me, but you have been so much more. You have been a friend. You didn't judge . . . well, maybe a few times that were merited . . . but you allowed me to express myself without suggesting or forcing me to be like anyone else. You saw the diamond in the rough that may not be evident to those with a naked eye. Your hard truth was always easier to digest with the kindness you gave with it, and for that, I will be eternally grateful. You nurtured my personal and professional growth—never allowing me to sell myself short. You challenged me to look beyond the obstacles and see opportunity."

I was not alone in my experience with Lynn. All sponsors benefited as well—an unintended outcome but a valuable one, nonetheless. The program elicited an enriching sense of obligation and commitment.

Even the selection process of both sponsors and partners was unique in varied ways. Although the program initially targeted high-performing or high-risk team members to boost their sense of belonging, it grew to reach a much broader group. Additionally, true to our commitment of one conversation at a time, we made certain the process was as personal as possible. Rather than a group email telling varied people they'd been selected as sponsors and that orientation begins Friday, we spoke one-on-one with the selected sponsors and with their assigned team members to offer specifics of the assignment and to address any questions they might have.

As the program grew in popularity, we maintained our focus on who we included in the formal sponsorship program, using a comprehensive set of criteria and a review process to better ensure equity. Sometimes, the answer to an applicant was, in fact, "no" or "not yet." But in those cases, we also made those personal phone calls to those not selected. We partnered them with a different set of supports, sometimes informal sponsors, coaches, or a mentor. We gave them advice and other forms of guidance. Our thinking was that if someone had the initiative to at least apply, we made certain to follow up. They might not be in the formal program, but we made sure they got additional resources, input, and feedback.

In many ways, our sponsorship and advocacy program was important in that it simply acknowledged reality. For one thing, the initiative recognized that many such sponsorship relationships already existed throughout the firm, although they were largely organic. The rub was that, while certain segments of the company would naturally have access to such informal relationships, far too many others did not, specifically women and people of color.

The fact that we identified these gaps was and remains vitally important because they exist in most organizations. By introducing a formal sponsorship program, we were merely interrupting a traditional system to provide a far greater range of impact. It embodied the essential truth that, when you grow in an organization, you do it through the help of others. Moreover, every organization has a set of unwritten rules of how they operate and why certain processes are followed. Through our sponsorship program, we looked to boost the number of people with access to that information so that those unwritten rules and norms were no longer an obstacle for any team member.

Another reality we acknowledged was the importance of recognizing the greater meaning of work. We discovered from many of our team members who were women or people of color that there was a prevailing mindset, not unique to HORNE, that if you keep your nose to the grindstone and work hard, you will inevitably advance in both your career and the company. Mary Bennett, our consultant helping with diversity and inclusion, had shared this particular insight: many women frequently assume that, if they work hard and keep their head down, they will be noticed and fairly rewarded.

To that end, Charles Curry poured out his heart to us in one meeting that evolved into tears and hugs, as he shared that, many times, he felt he had to work longer and harder for the same or less recognition.

When you hear these experiences from a team member who is both admired and loved, it literally shakes you. Every belief and assumption about right and wrong are turned upside down. I'm sitting across from a man I admire and love, who I always give the benefit of good intentions. This is someone I recruited to be on our government services team. I was shaking because, even though he intellectually knew all of those things, his life experiences would not allow him to have the confidence to believe it. Deep down, he felt he had to do more than anyone else to have the same opportunities. "That's just the way it is," he said to me.

It shook me as I heard those words and realized how much courage Charles had to muster to have a conversation that I had viewed as collaboration between team members. We realized that every team member's experiences and perceptions drastically affect how they grow to trust and have an inner peace that, yes, they truly belong. That sense of belonging frees them to be everything God intended them to be.

How could we be so blind to some of these perceptions of people we worked with every day? Was it simply another coincidence that Charles was on our team and had the courage to trust us even prior to our embracing the Wise Firm? He persisted even before we began the journey to understand.

What are the odds that we could have a team member with so much love, grace, and courage to help lead us to beBetter? Once more, God, faith, and culture intersected in our story. Maybe another "coincidence"?

(By the way, if Charles said a prayer at one of our team meetings, you pretty much felt like you could skip church on Sunday. He was a strong man of faith and demonstrated our commitment to love and care in every interaction.)

Not only did our sponsorship program acknowledge and leverage the fact that you need the help of others to advance, but it also recognized that simply keeping your head down and grinding it out isn't necessarily the best career plan. Instead, our sponsors would point their protégés toward work of particular significance, such as projects closely connected to the strategic objectives of the company. In effect, sponsors helped ensure that their protégés continued to work hard but made sure to include activities of genuine career value.

Just as valuable, the sponsorship and advocacy program also proactively addressed a challenge that we truly did not foresee at the outset—the role of support and guidance for remote teammates. Although we beat COVID-19 to the punch, so to speak, by encouraging remote work prior to the pandemic, COVID-19's boost to untraditional work arrangements highlighted the issue of assisting teammates who weren't just down the hall or in the next office. By emphasizing committed, personal relationships, the sponsorship initiative proved well suited to supporting all teammates no matter where they happened to work. No one was left on an island without an important network of connection.

A growing number of remote employees also reflected our commitment to consistent flexibility. In so doing, we worked to ensure one of the central pillars of the Wise Firm—making certain that fearless, unrivaled flexibility would never be construed as the privilege of a special few. By ensuring flexibility for all, we effectively slayed another guilt vampire—the sense that some were receiving breaks and opportunities denied others. We worked at every step to make certain flexibility was truly universal.

As I wrap up this section on sponsorship and advocacy, it's essential that I salute the contribution of Mary Bennett, one of the consultants who walked with us along our journey for many years in true partnership; her role in helping these varied components proved so successful. Mary took the time to learn about our goals and values and was instrumental in developing and implementing the overall sponsorship program. Lacking her input, the journey would have only been that much more challenging. Mary taught us so many of the best practices that we share and use to this day.

The sponsorship program remains a reflection of our commitment to building high performance—achievement and growth available to everyone at HORNE, not just a select few. It solidified our commitment that we want everyone to see and have the opportunity to reach their full potential.

EXPRESSING LOVE AND CARE WITH FEEDBACK

Now, this may seem like an odd segue, but bear with me. One of the specific things we learned in our early conversations about belonging (or the lack thereof) was that we were really not great at feedback. I'm not talking about the once- or twice-a-year performance reviews; I mean *real* feedback that was honest and that helped team members feel appreciated and cared for. We were bad at the kind of feedback that helped our people know where they stood. This was the kind of information you share because you love and care about someone else's success, that you learn to ask for so you can grow and serve clients better, and that transforms teams. I'll be blunt: we were really bad at that.

Sure, we had formal review processes, but we needed much more to drive both belonging and better career ownership. What we needed was in no way a checkbox, superficial program. We needed a mindset shift. This was about having better, more focused conversations. That was a big swing. On top of that, over time, we found that not every role in the firm matched well with all the attributes that we intended to measure. It made evaluations that much more challenging.

We finally had to admit to ourselves that performance advisors weren't really great at being performance advisors. Accordingly, we knew we had to get better at giving and receiving feedback and making it actionable. Again, we needed to have better conversations.

Although we clearly recognized we needed to go in a fresh direction in our feedback skills, it was another coincidence that helped steer us down the right path. A career coach in the firm passed along a book he happened to pick up at the airport called *Thanks for the Feedback*. The authors are Sheila Heen and Doug Stone, both rock stars who are part of the Harvard Negotiation Project, which examines innovative ideas to improve negotiation and conflict resolution.

That really flipped the script. Instead of having our performance advisors plow through conventional training that emphasizes how to give feedback, we went opposite. Every employee in the company went through a half-day workshop on how to receive feedback. In particular, that training separated feedback into three distinct forms—appreciation, coaching, and evaluation. Absolutely game changing.

As a result, performance advisors came to understand that every team member needed all three parts to truly provide effective and actionable feedback. Additionally, everyone came to understand that feedback is not an annual performance review. Rather, feedback should take place every day in conversations of all sorts. Moreover, advisors gained a better grasp of the varied goals of coaching, such as coaching for performance as opposed to coaching for career development.

It was a significant shift but one that reinforced our mission to build a sense of belonging by having better, more meaningful conversations. It also built a core of empowered people and results as it helped empower teammates to seek out the feedback they needed, not just wait for it. And it taught them to recognize when they were getting poor or inappropriate feedback and how to go about pursuing more meaningful guidance.

ASK, UNDERSTAND, GROW

The complete transformation on how we offered and received feedback prompted Chrissy Leggett to share her thoughts and experiences in a culture blog:

"These days, as I walk down the halls at HORNE, I repeatedly hear 'Thanks for the feedback!' It's a common saying these days. I think about how feedback has impacted our culture, and I smile in gratitude.

"As we discussed, not very long before, our culture was overrun with conflict avoidance. We were afraid to ask for feedback, not knowing what to do with any feedback we might receive. Team members would rather not say anything at all than speak the truth in love. Feedback was something you got once a year, twice if you were lucky, in your annual evaluation. Coaching feedback was fleeting. One time, I heard about a supervisor who wasn't pleased with a team member's work. Instead of giving points on how to be better, she ripped up the work papers, threw them on the floor, and said, 'Do it again.' And appreciation feedback was even more of an elusive unicorn. We walked around with blinders on and arms crossed—unwilling to be vulnerable or open to growth.

"But then came the day when we dug into what Belonging at HORNE really means. How can we make our sense of belonging stronger? We started connecting the dots between conflict avoidance and giving and receiving feedback well.

"What a watershed moment for this firm! We learned that there's no one-size-fits-all approach to giving feedback and spent time developing a 'Guide to Working with Me' to share our preferences for receiving feedback. This feedback movement has given us a common language as we journey the Wise Firm way with a continuous growth philosophy.

"Three strategies have helped me in my feedback quest: ask, understand, and grow:

"Ask. Since we have this common language, I feel empowered to ask for the feedback that I want and need—even the specific type of feedback that I need (appreciation, coaching, or evaluation)! Asking for feedback helps me reduce the blind spots in my life.

"Understand. If I don't understand the feedback, I ask questions that peel back the layers and get to the true heart of the feedback. This has been a mindset change for me! I've moved from an instinctual 'that's wrong' to a 'tell me more' reaction. And if coaching feedback is what I need, I've learned that any piece of feedback can be turned into a coaching session by opening up, digging in, and asking questions.

"Grow. I use feedback as an opportunity to learn something, knowing that I'm not stuck and can grow to obtain better results—to have a stance of open-handed vulnerability instead of cross-armed defensiveness.

"Feedback is a life-changing way to beEvenBetter. I encourage you to take these three strategies and see how you can use them in your feedback quest.

"Thanks for the feedback, HORNE!"

—Insights from HORNE team member blog

A BASKETFUL OF MAGNETIC MOMENTS

Courage was at its finest in 2020, when we introduced Circles of Belonging to our team. The board of directors and the Belonging task force had been listening and was concerned about the very real problem of racism and prejudice against our country's Black and African American citizens.

Early on, Alethia Thomas's influence and constructive voice helped us understand that we could not check the box or ignore the pain that was being experienced by these team members. We wanted our firm to be part of the solution rather than a cheerleader on the sidelines. We knew the pain of racism was deep, not just a flare-up from recent events; our Black and African American team members were living with this pain daily. We wanted to beBetter within our team. We knew this wasn't about a new program. We needed to listen. We needed to try to understand. We needed better awareness. We aspired to help all of us move forward together. Our board felt the urgency to act.

The Circles of Belonging were designed for eight to ten team members to voluntarily convene in a private space where they would begin conversations to listen to each other, to learn from each other's experiences, and to move forward together. We focused particularly on the pain and experiences of our Black and African American team members.

We knew we could not go down this path unprepared. We needed facilitators to lead each group. In addition to listening and learning, we wanted to be able to confidentially summarize what HORNE could do better and put an action plan in place to create a stronger sense of belonging.

We called in one of our champions, one of our fast friends, an advisor and previous keynote speaker on culture, Kimberly Ellison-Taylor. What a joy and what energy she brings to helping others have safe places to collaborate in conversations that make a difference. These safe spaces lead to better listening and understanding.

Working with a number of leaders, including several board members, Kimberly led us in training over several weeks. Actually, I'm not sure "training" accurately conveys how she led us. She guided us toward deeper understanding in a way that allowed us to hear old mottos with new meaning. We spent time defining and unpacking words like *racism*, for example. We understood in a new way that racism is much wider in breadth than we'd previously considered, realizing it is a daily pain for many of our team members who are people of color. It is a way of life, where we (certainly me) previously confined it to a specific single act or bad actor. We realized that true listening is really not about fixing, at least not at first. Instead, real listening is demonstrating empathy for the person's pain, including past pain to them or their family or their entire people group, and it is part of the healing process. Now, we firmly believe that being heard by someone who cares is part of growing courage and trust, to face racism together.

We grew in our understanding that a sense of belonging for a person of color team member takes more courage on their part, as they must extend trust in a world where their experience has been very different. The role of individual leaders at the local level has significant impact and must contribute to the psychological safety required for a real sense of belonging. As we help others have a strong sense of belonging, we have the awareness that it will, at times, be different for some people of color team members. For example, as a Black professor once shared with me, if I am giving feedback to a person of color team member, intentional trust and care must be established for the feedback to be beneficial. Their upbringing might create perceptions that make the feedback untrustworthy.

Kimberly connected ideologies and perceptions and frankly but lovingly helped us see how we all contribute to the problem, even if unintentionally. Our life experiences and our upbringing generate wide variances in beliefs and perceptions around many topics, interactions, and words. Being situationally aware is critical. Growing awareness of various triggers is part of the educational process to better connections.

We can't be ignorant or unconcerned of others' experiences, and we learned we have to invest time, trust, and vulnerability in that process. Silence and ignoring the pain of racism creates a void in trust that destroys the ability for every team member to have that strong sense of belonging. We concluded our training with a day together to practice many of the things that we had covered.

Thanks to Kimberly's sage advice, love, and prayers, our leaders showed the courage to step into these circles and lead our team members to great connections, understanding, and a sense of belonging for all team members. We guided the conversations to attempt to hear experiences within our firm. We didn't want to focus on areas beyond our control, but we did want to own what we could impact. So we attempted to understand the unspoken issues and behaviors in our firm that stifle the sense of belonging for our Black and African American team members.

But it wasn't the trained facilitators who were the champions of the Circles of Belonging. We may have been brave enough to ask the questions, but the team members who chose to participate were far more courageous to share their answers. I participated in two of the circles. The sheer pain, tears, and care that were demonstrated changed all of us. I cannot imagine the courage it took for our Black and African American team members to show up and share their realities.

Let me be completely upfront. We didn't know if this idea would work. But we trusted that the foundation that had been laid for almost a decade would stand firm. And it did. It was another example where everyone leads, as we had team members summon the courage to step into the circles and learn from each other. The Circles of Belonging were and are game changers.

BUILDING FUN TRADITIONS

It was hardly an issue of all work and no play during this period of transition and growth. In fact, it was anything but that! For one thing, however challenging and even intimidating all this change may have been at the time, it was a genuinely fun time to be a part of the experience. Not only did people recognize the great things we could achieve the more we were united in our efforts, but the greater the number of team members who embraced the vision we had offered, the more the energy built. You could feel it every day—a magnetic positive energy and a joy to be part of something bigger than ourselves.

Being intentional is a big aspect of building fun and joy in the workplace. It goes back to the ability for leadership to demonstrate beyond words, appreciation, respect, recognition, and caring. Another significant investment by our board and partners—people before profit—was the position of event planner. When it came to our internal firm events, meetings, and partner meetings, our event planner, Leslie Petro, was our champion, leading our strategies to make it fun, connecting, engaging, and first class. She is a remarkable talent who is using her talents today to elevate our team event experiences to world class. Our purpose, as I shared with Leslie all the way back to 2011, was that everyone at HORNE should feel VIP and special when we plan an event. Leslie and her volunteers have wowed us time after time.

To further our magnetic energy, I took it upon myself to play a somewhat personal role in spreading our vision. I would pass out $100 bills to anyone who could recite our vision verbatim. In the interest of thoroughness, here it is, word for word:

> *"We deliver unrivaled, focused expertise.*
> *We collaborate to proactively guide and serve our people,*
> *clients, and communities to reach their full potential."*

It came as no surprise to me that, as the company-wide effort took hold, I was handing out more and more $100 bills. In fact, the exercise became so pervasive that new hires would start their HORNE career with the phrase memorized to perfection. We created a page on our website to celebrate the winners. Although my wallet was considerably lighter, it was rewarding to see how many people took the message captured by our vision to heart—newcomers as well as established teammates.

Then there was the birth of Sunday lunch—a concept for which we have Scott Keller to thank. Scott, who is a leader in our government services division, had been working as an outside consultant for us before we were able to convince him to come on board. In our early discussions, Scott observed that whenever he interacted with our team or shared a meal with a HORNE team member—be it any meal of the day or on any day in the week—to him, it felt like Sunday lunch. By that, he meant a warm, friendly environment with others, sharing laughter and stories, as so many families and friends do at Sunday lunch. It had little if any similarity to stiff and formal business lunches.

The phrase caught on, and soon people throughout the company were referring to gatherings with colleagues and teammates as "Sunday lunch." The term is still in use to this day. I'm excited to share that, in many of these Sunday lunches, the team also offered up a prayer of gratitude. These prayers helped our team members stay in touch with how much God had blessed our firm and all of the things we had to be thankful for. Remember—gratitude generates magnetic energy. It's contagious.

It may seem cosmetic, but the Sunday lunch phenomenon truly showed that we were on the right road in our journey toward the Wise Firm—a journey characterized not only by practical progress but by a shared joy and enthusiasm. We were beginning to see the power of traditions in working to build a culture.

But fun traditions were not limited to our Sunday lunch celebrations. As Meridith Elliott Powell, a consultant who worked with us in a variety of capacities noted in a blog, we were more than happy to take our fun traditions movement right down to the street—as it happened, in New Orleans:

> This event began like no other Leadership Summit I have ever attended. It began with a full second-line parade down the middle of Canal Street and continued all the way to the House of Blues. Just so you get the full picture, the entire team of HORNE literally took over Canal Street with a full band, full parade, and a full-on march, making a big splash in the Big Easy. Once at the House of Blues, it was a celebration, great food, an amazing band, and a show—HORNE's got talent! And while I could talk and tell stories for hours about this kickoff event, what I learned was the importance and value of taking the time and investing in building community. See, Joey, HORNE's executive partner, and the team of HORNE understand what they gain when they encourage their team to connect, have fun, and build relationships outside of the work environment. I think one of the HORNE team members said it best when I asked him about working

at HORNE. His answer was: "We are a family, and the more
we play together, the better relationships we build, the more
productive we are."[9]

With so many remote team members and a steady diet of hybrid sched-
ules focused around working from home, fun and connecting become a
bigger and bigger challenge. Intentionality is the key word here: we must
be intentional to promote opportunities for connection and to plan fun
events that stretch over the internet and pull people together.

Technology plays a huge role for connection and is the tool that keeps
our collaborative energy flowing. We cannot encourage others enough to
invest in tools that improve collaboration—faster internet, unrestricted
video conferencing, larger high-resolution monitors, better headsets, and
higher-quality cameras. How are you optimizing tools such as Microsoft
Teams, Slack, Google Chat, or Zoom? What is your intranet, and how
can you design log-ons to promote easy access to your in-house version of
Facebook? We can all boost teamwork, connection, fun, and productivity
by giving team members the tools and the space to connect, collaborate,
and celebrate with a good time. Magnetic cultures find creative ways to
span the gap of remote team members.

As they say, actions speak louder than words, and data demonstrate
our results. By 2017, five years into building the Wise Firm, 94 percent of
our team members said they felt a strong sense of belonging at HORNE.
Within that statistic, 92 percent felt like they were making a difference,
and 88 percent said they had increased their leadership responsibilities with
the firm, as well as increased leadership responsibilities with clients.

Perhaps even more important, it was also clear that our commitment to
loving and caring was truly helping build better lives. I'll leave it to Charles
Curry, once more, to summarize it perfectly: "You being in my life, a part

---

9   Meridith Elliott Powell, "Unrivaled, Fearless, Flexibility: Three Strategies to Create Full Team Engagement,"
     Meridith Elliott Powell (blog), September 1, 2022, https://www.meridithelliottpowell.com/unrivaled-fearless-
     flexibility.

of my world, is greatly enriching me. You are helping me to grow beyond my wildest dreams and prayers. Working together, who knows what mountains we will move or the lands we shall conquer? I can't express how much you are blessing me. Thanks for putting up with me as I work to beBetter. Thank you for all you're doing."

||||||||||||||||||||||||||||||||||||||||||||||||||||||||||||||||||||||||||||||||||||||||||||||||||||||||||

MAGNETIC THOUGHTS

"Dear children, let us not love with words or speech,
but with actions and in truth."

—1 JOHN 3:18 NIV

- Love and care are central to building a strong sense of belonging. Respect, appreciation, recognition, coaching, and investment of time all demonstrate a loving and caring culture for people.

- A belonging task force such as the one we employed at HORNE can be particularly effective in addressing significant issues and challenges with a diverse and committed membership—far more effective than simply designating one person or an existing department such as human resources.

- The Belonging task force and its annual reporting of transparency on our goals and progress have become a foundation for HORNE's lasting commitment to transparency and accountability.

- It's essential to acknowledge that every organization has unwritten rules that impact career growth. Our sponsorship program broadened access to those. Formal sponsorship and advocacy programs are game changers for high-risk team members.

- We chose to use the term *sponsors* rather than *mentors* for our one-on-one program. Sponsors have skin in the game; they have to believe in their protégés.

- Feedback is part of caring and helping team members reach their full potential. Powerful, effective feedback is more about the conversation than a score. Find ways to help team members to understand and seek feedback.

- Team members have a stronger sense of belonging when they know where they stand, how they are doing, and how to move forward in their career.

- Our Circles of Belonging brought together people from all sorts of different backgrounds and provided a place to bravely share life experiences with others. Hiring a training expert helped move the teams forward into greater understanding of others.

- Being silent on racism leads to people of color team members feeling unheard, which leads to a lack of trust.

- Among other fun traditions we cultivated at HORNE were Sunday lunches, which referred to fun, informal meals—any day of the week—workers shared together. Many team members start these meals with prayers of thanks because we believe gratitude generates magnetic energy.

- Magnetic cultures find creative ways to span the gap of remote team members, whether that means supporting more resources in the office or expanding those for remote workers in their homes.

7

Full Potential— but Not without Some Pain

ONE OF THE BEDROCKS THAT carried us through the birth and growth of the Wise Firm was the complete embrace of the principle that no one reaches their full potential alone. That idea manifested itself in any number of ways. It appeared in sponsorship, in full potential coaching, in one-on-one conversations about belonging, in feedback conversations about career progression, and in personal stories as team members shared how they advanced. I know as our journey toward the Wise Firm continued, it became evident how much we needed help from each other to maintain our courage and confidence that we were, in fact, pursuing the right course.

For many, that help came from others within HORNE. For me, it also came from a much greater source—yet another coincidence of God, faith, and culture.

HOW TO CHANGE A MINDSET

One positive result that has served us well since turning our journey over to God was the realization that there are simply a number of things we can exert precious little control over. One such valuable lesson involves people's mindsets.

I recently came across a quotation from Dr. Martin Luther King Jr. that truly resonates with me: "Change does not roll in on the wheels of inevitability but comes through continuous struggle." That's as true with the fight to secure equality for all citizens as it is with reinventing a company. No culture reaches its potential with simply a vision. People have to see it to truly embrace it. At HORNE, there were a large number of people who, in fact, did see the vision that we had. They were fully committed to building toward the potential the vision held.

But although we were well into the firm's reinvention—and positive results were beginning to take place—there were others who didn't necessarily see it. Conceptually, they may have understood it, but there wasn't the complete, driving commitment that we needed.

There seem to always be roughly four different groups when it comes to resistance. Some simply disagree with the general direction. Although we had more evidence and magnetic energy than when we started, we had team members that did not buy in.

I label the next group *I paid my dues!* A member of this group might say, "This is all about respect, and I helped grow this firm to this stage. I should have more input." Here is where we encouraged them to have their voice heard today as we needed them to help pull the rope.

We are all familiar with the third group; I know I hang out here too often. This group just wants to do what they did yesterday. They just want to do their work and go home. It's the status quo bias or camping bias, where things are good enough right now so let's just coast, maybe set up camp and stay awhile. With this group, we must continue to stress the great risk this poses to the entire firm, to ignore hard trends and to procrastinate on things that we know will make us better.

Much of the hesitancy or resistance (the biggest group, by the way) came down to an age-old concern that has often hindered meaningful change—that we were simply changing too much, too fast. Although this was the largest group of resisters, it was also a group that had helped move us forward. They had simply hit the wall on how much change they wanted to tolerate. We addressed this mindset by flipping the question around.

In periods of incremental change, it's perfectly reasonable to be concerned about going too fast. The issue was that *we were not in a time of incremental change*; we were in truly transformational times. From the technology we use to most every element of our daily lives, we were experiencing exponential change unlike the world had ever experienced before. And this was all pre-pandemic.

Accordingly, we reflected on an alternative question: Are we moving fast enough? Rather than too much too soon, are we changing with sufficient speed? That is where the greatest risk is. It's a core question of keeping up or being left behind. Flipping the question as we did made the concern about going too fast rather moot.

We also reflected on these questions to augment the discussion:

- What would have to be true for us to change direction?

- What key performance indicators are we measuring that actually may be slowing us down?

- Does our pricing genuinely reflect our worth, our impact?

- My Amazon question: Will our present business model survive exponential change by new competitors? Phrased another way, what are the odds that our services could beat an all-encompassing entity such as Amazon?

Those were the questions that we used when the pushback began to slow us down or darken our pathway forward. And, in turn, it led to more conversations that included new information—issues that allowed many to question and even change many of their beliefs and assumptions as to what we were attempting to do.

When it comes to culture or exponential growth, I love to reflect on the wise words of scientist and professor Richard Feynman: "The first principle is that you must not fool yourself—and you are the easiest person to fool."[10]

However challenging and frustrating the experience or the reason behind the resistance, it taught us all an essential truth. You really can't change people's mindsets. A change in mindset simply can't be mandated. If people are afraid of change, they will continue to make up objections even as you work hard to overcome them. All you can do is offer sufficient information, encourage an open mind, and keep inviting them to come along beside you.

Individuals have to make the choice. That choice usually only happens as two things become apparent—firsthand experience and celebrating progress on the journey. The latter helps people learn more about the benefits of the culture shift and highlights the opportunity for them to be part of it. As more progress is evident, not only do more team members become engaged and contribute to building a better culture, but it also becomes more unnerving to stay locked in the status quo. In fact, people begin to worry about missing out on something that is clearly working and generating some newfound energy.

Only people can change their mindset. This is the only way to influence those choices.

THE CHOICE

As I said, one of the most valuable lessons we received when confronted with those concerned about changing too quickly was that you simply can't force-feed change. It's up to the individual

---

10   Farnam Street Media, "Who Is Richard Feynman? The Curious Character Who Mastered Thinking and Physics," FS.blog, March 1, 2020, https://fs.blog/intellectual-giants/richard-feynman.

to choose to change. This affected our foundational sense of belonging also as it is really every team member's choice if they want to embrace a sense of belonging and if they want to help others grow their sense of belonging even stronger.

As it happened, a HORNE team member touched on this very topic in a guest blog. This teammate, long situated in New York, had been reassigned back to our Jackson, Mississippi, office. Anxious about how he would fit in after the relocation, he came to realize that wasn't a matter of some sort of external force; the choice was entirely up to him. As he writes in the blog,

"Still, super anxious about the unknowns of being back, I had a choice. I could be super sad and feel like everything was starting on a terrible note, or I could choose to, once again, not assume the worst. The Ridgeland office had once been a place that felt like my second home, but now it was making me feel so anxious and scared. I had been away for four years and wasn't sure how I would adjust.

"Trying to establish a sense of belonging sometimes is a challenge and harder when you see a bunch of new faces and even some team members you have known for years but haven't been around in a long time. I worried about how to reengage and what my first steps should be. I hesitated to be as open and dare to lead in a place that I hadn't been in quite some time.

"It wasn't long before I realized that I must take the first step and be more engaging with team members, both new and existing, if I wanted to feel that same sense of belonging. As a team member, management, or partner, we must not forget that we all feel vulnerable at times. We get so caught up in our work that we forget to remain engaged. Reengaging isn't easy. I must do my part to create a sense of belonging that I also wish to have.

"Once I began to reengage and speak to team members daily,

continued

I would find common ground to initiate conversation, and I began to feel more connected. I quickly saw how my sense of belonging was growing. I was talking to team members and they were talking to me. I could have come back into the office with my guard up, but I chose not to, and I'm so glad I didn't. Now, I look for every opportunity to talk with new team members, new faces, or existing ones to help them build their sense of belonging."

—Insights from HORNE team member blog

FULL POTENTIAL COACHING

Our effort to empower the doubters among us reinforced how compelling it was to understand that no one can move forward without the help of others. In the case of the "too fast, too soon" folks, it involved turning the question around to help them solidify their confidence that we were, in fact, on the right path.

However, when it came to the more practical nature of that dynamic—what we could do to help people develop faster and better advance in their careers—we were stumped. Looking far and wide in our profession, we simply did not see an answer. So we expanded our search to other professional service firms.

We hit pay dirt. We found a small engineering company that had implemented internal coaches for all professional staff to help them advance faster and better navigate their careers. Our board, never shy to try something new, put the plan into action.

Thus was born the idea and execution of full potential coaching. Starting with just one career coach at the outset of the program, we've since built a team of coaches who are actively assisting teammates with any challenges or issues they may be confronting.

At a glance, full potential coaching might not seem all that different from our sponsorship program. But there are significant distinctions. For one thing, coaching places a greater emphasis on helping team members solve their own problems. It slants toward personal ownership and greater responsibility on the participants' part, where sponsorship is also taking into account the organizational dynamics or broader challenges that may be contributing to an employee's professional barriers. Coaching is definitely geared to equipping teammates with tools with which they can better navigate their work and careers more autonomously.

Furthermore, as the name implies, full potential coaching was and is geared to maximizing a person's skills and abilities. That, too, can differ somewhat from a sponsor's responsibilities, which are often geared to providing access, company knowledge, opportunities, and political capital.

Additionally, full potential coaching operates on a strict regimen of confidentiality. While sponsorship activities could be a bit more public— for instance, we made it a point to visibly celebrate sponsorship success stories—the specifics of any full potential coaching relationship remain private. That boosts participants' comfort level and willingness to share delicate, personal details and information. We eventually even separated it from our HR function to guarantee coaching conversations never hindered the performance cycle, real or perceived.

Finally, we were taking the additional step of hiring full-time, professionally trained coaches—not just adding coaching to an existing employee's training. We wanted people whose full-time responsibility was coaching. That intentional emphasis further boosted the power and influence of the program. Coaching is another very visible means of behaviors and systems that demonstrate a caring for each team member to accomplish their dreams and seek their full potential.

COACHING IS A GAME CHANGER

Not surprisingly, full potential coaching has proved to be an absolute game changer in a number of areas. Initially, we provided the coaching at certain stages in a team member's career. Ultimately, it evolved into providing it on a team member's request—completely voluntary. We did not create any silos or differentiate our team members by race, gender, generation, or other lenses to access the coaching. This further strengthened our sense of belonging. Additionally, participant feedback has been outstanding, with team members consistently reporting that their coaching experience has proved effective at helping them achieve their goals.

One teammate put it very well: "I felt secluded. Moving to another firm or company at the time was the only option for me, but then came my full potential coach. He has been such a blessing to me. Immediately, he allowed me the opportunity to communicate the truth about my experiences at HORNE. By doing this, he was able to shed some light on my situation. Through my continuous communications with him, I have grown to take full ownership of my career. I have taken the initiative to meet with other leaders, who have helped me tremendously."

Interestingly enough, full potential coaching also showed the value of teammate reassignment. Once coaching started, we began shifting people around the firm more often because we were discovering through the coaching process that some teammates simply weren't in the right place to achieve all that they could. Rather than simply losing them or settling for substandard performance, we increasingly moved people into different roles and to different teams throughout the firm. It wasn't a matter of what they were doing so much as who they were doing it with. Accordingly, we became that much more open about finding teammates the best spot for them.

As with other programs geared to guiding and assisting all HORNE teammates, we emphasized from the outset that utilizing a coach for help was not a sign of weakness. Rather, it reflected both candor and courage—the candor to recognize that someone else might be able to help and the courage to actually ask for it.

Looking in the mirror can often be uncomfortable, but full potential coaching empowered any number of teammates to look themselves squarely in the eye and recognize what they needed to grow. The partners openly shared that they used coaching to help them reach their full potential.

Almost every year, we had 25 to 50 percent of our partners actively being coached by an external or internal coach to help them play to a strength or eliminate a restraint.

The last benefit—yet another coincidence—that we gained due to no planning of our own was tremendous insights into how desperately we needed to improve our performance advisors' skills and messaging. We were able to institute lots of best practices and training, which raised our effectiveness with performance and career navigation feedback.

Once again, every journey to greatness requires multiple leaders who own a future vision and lead accordingly. Our first champion was Steve Carter, a former Big Four director, who helped us evolve from an idea to implementing a program that impacted people in its very first year. Dr. Joe Paul is another such champion, having had the tough job of coaching me in my early years in the partnership. Joe Paul came aboard early to provide experience and wisdom to the program.

Additionally, our first certified coach, Tara Chrisco, came aboard. It's always magnetic when amazing talent chooses to join the vision of building the Wise Firm. Tara immediately assumed a leadership role and became a champion of coaching for our full potential with individual team members, the board, and with our entire firm. Under her direction, the program took off, and we never looked back. Champions can operate like this when you have magnetic energy with high trust.

Today, she leads our internal and external coaching and leadership development teams. Tara was instrumental in helping plan and execute our managing partner transition, which began in 2020 and was successfully transitioned in May 2021.

FIERCE OWNERSHIP

Here's some sage advice from our full potential coach Joe Paul in reference to the power and value of a 100 percent responsibility mindset:

continued

"To me, fierce ownership is showing up every day with uncommon discipline and acting on every action, opportunity, or request as though you personally—literally—owned your practice group, even as though you owned the firm! It is putting the needs and best interests of your clients, colleagues, and the firm before your own.

"Fierce ownership is both a mindset and a discipline. By looking at results as if you are 100 percent responsible and others have no responsibility at all, you become empowered rather than dependent on other people and events you do not control. Blaming and justifying—those two things are among the greatest wastes of human time and energy. The 100 percent responsibility mindset is the way to free yourself of useless blaming and justifying and, from there, stay in the game exhibiting fierce ownership to get the desired result."

Which brings me to the following question: What is going on in our culture that we are not taking fierce ownership of?

—*Insights from HORNE team member blog*

RECRUITING TO ACHIEVE 10 PERCENT PLUS

The further we ventured on our journey toward the Wise Firm, it was becoming increasingly evident that the outcome of the effort rested not only with leadership—however critical that naturally was—but with each and every individual throughout the company. What level of success we were able to achieve hinged on their shared mindset, their magnetic energy to voluntarily and consistently go above and beyond, and their commitment to beBetter, day in and day out.

That posed two distinct but related challenges. First was having a sufficient number of people to carry out the company's reinvention. It was also a matter of making as certain as possible that we not only had enough people but also those with the mindset eager to embrace the vision of the Wise Firm. (As I shared earlier, we had identified the hard trends indicating that we would have a significant shortage of talent over the next five to ten years.)

Accordingly, in yet another pivot away from business as usual, we established the goal of building a staff that was 10 percent over capacity. As the pandemic hit, by coincidence, we were in a better position to respond to the blue ocean of needs from our clients. It was not a great position necessarily but better than if we had taken a management position of being lean and optimizing utilization.

Our shared experience in building the Wise Firm to this point was that, while there were some focus areas where we were inconsistent with our growth, there were others that performed far better. So, to achieve the exponential growth that we sought, we knew we needed sufficient people-power to make that happen.

There was some expected and obvious short-term discomfort. After all, if you have 10 percent people on board more than you need at the moment, that's bound to affect the bottom line. And, with us, it did. But, more important, over the long term, the precise opposite was true. By making excess staffing the rule rather than the exception, we were positioned to take on larger projects and grow that much faster. Just as valuable, excess staffing allowed both the time and the resources for innovation. It provided greater opportunities for whiteboarding and "What's possible?" ideas. Furthermore, with a larger number of people involved, there was less risk of burnout, of repeatedly wearing your best team members out. We simply had more people pulling on the rope.

It proved to be a key driver in our push to grow from a good culture to a great one. Investment is always essential in any significant undertaking. Even though we didn't always get things right, even though growth stretched us almost constantly and poor decisions on short-term focus grabbed us too frequently, overall having that extra 10 percent target helped get us over many hills.

But not just any additional 10 percent. Up to this point in time, most of the ideas and effort behind the development of the Wise Firm had been internally focused. Ultimately, though, we realized that it was time to take the Wise Firm beyond the confines of our four walls. It was becoming increasingly evident that, as had been our intent from day one, our culture was a differentiator—a way to set ourselves apart as an employer, where people would enjoy a singular experience. Accordingly, we began to build external messaging to help attract the sort of people who would not only thrive in such an environment but who would also have the mindset and commitment to help build the sort of firm we were trying to achieve.

We developed a comprehensive recruiting strategy, including videos and other material. We had confidence that it would prove effective, given a shift in what people were looking for in their careers. It aligned with many of the core issues that we had been developing internally—purpose, mission, bedrock values, a strong sense of belonging, giving back to the community, and career progression.

Furthermore, we leveraged the blossoming magnetic energy that we saw growing consistently within the firm—the discretionary effort, the mindset of voluntarily thinking that naturally drives people to stay an hour late and make certain they get things right or generate the courage to challenge the status quo. We started releasing it externally into the marketplace. That positive, magnetic energy, that sense of belonging began to make our recruiting efforts significantly better. It also strengthened our retention. Our ability to message who we were had genuine definition. It was truly compelling.

Our pivot in how we recruited also reflected an acknowledgment regarding mindsets that I noted earlier. It was a simple truth. People are either intrinsically or externally motivated. It's as simple as that. Some, who are externally motivated, are the "campers"—those with a defined threshold of how far they could be motivated or who stop at the first barrier they encounter. On the other hand, intrinsically motivated individuals, the folks you give the tools to, who you offer support to, who you provide with the resources and then kind of get out of their way—those were the people our shift in recruiting was focused on. Neil Forbes, my successor as managing partner, had the vision to identify this gap and take on the challenge to find a better way to screen talent that would thrive in a high-performance culture. His due diligence with Disney (he is a big fan, by the way) led us to adopt criteria and interview techniques to enhance our ability to identify these go-getters.

It was so successful that, since that point, it's been a recruiting standard at HORNE that every applicant needs to pass a motivation-based interview. We knew we wanted people with strong and inherent motivation. Accordingly, we took steps to make certain that those issues were covered before they spent day one with the company.

SENIORITY IS OUT THE WINDOW

With the pivot in our recruiting methodology and priorities, we were intentional in attracting the sort of people we wanted to contribute to the Wise Firm. Next up: how we measured how people performed once they were on board—or, rather, what we decided *not* to measure.

Those familiar with the accounting industry are all too familiar with the legacy KPIs for the profession—realization, utilization, and chargeable hours among them. However widely applied, they all produce pretty much the same sort of result: people focused on making their time sheet look good. Quantity, not necessarily quality or creativity.

Once more, we went opposite of the profession, starting with traditional KPI measurement. Rather than an emphasis on racking up as many utilization barometers as possible, we instead emphasized results. We encouraged people to ask themselves what they should be doing right now. What's the most valuable thing? Is what you're doing moving you toward the results that truly matter?

That was consistent with the shift toward results that we had implemented in other areas of the firm. Produce the results, and you will be rewarded accordingly.

We also introduced two additional philosophic and practical

changes—both of which ran absolutely counter to traditional industry practices. First was doing away with what could be described as "promotion season." By that, I mean the practice of setting aside particular times of the year in which promotions were handed out. No matter if a teammate had a particular career-shifting performance in, say, January and February, in our past, she might have to wait for another time in the year to receive a promotion based on that great work. To an outsider unfamiliar with the policy, that would seem utterly ludicrous—giving promotions a season, akin to hunting season or a particular time of year where certain production was at its peak. Those make sense; promotion season didn't even come close. Yet there it was, and it was all too commonly used, and we had certainly embraced it over the years.

Instead, we decided to reward results in real time. If somebody was ready for a promotion in March, they got a promotion in March. If somebody knocked it out of the park in October, they got a promotion in October.

That may sound like utter common sense, but it was often hard to get people's minds around the shift. For many, it was a significant change. We, like so many companies, had let the convenience and "efficiency" of the process overrule the best experience for our people.

But it made all the sense in the world to change. For one thing, having an immediate benefit for outstanding performance could only further fuel people's motivation to keep performing at their best. No more waiting around to see if the payoff would be there or not. Additionally, and just as important, it stood for our shift in priorities—putting people ahead of systems rather than the other way around.

Furthermore, it was also recognition that just because you have an established process, that doesn't necessarily mean that it's effective or is beneficial to the greatest number of people possible. It goes back once more to the shift that beBetter manifested. Being efficient at the wrong things couldn't possibly help build a Wise Firm.

Instead, it was all about results. And that naturally dovetailed into another against-the-grain policy shift. To put it bluntly, when it came to progressing in your career at HORNE, seniority was out the window.

That harkens back to another well-entrenched legacy in our profession—the proverbial seniority scorecard. So the thinking went, if you had 10 years under your belt at a particular company, you should be in line to make partner before anyone else with less experience. The mindset was locked in the perception that no one with fewer years could possibly be more ready than someone with longer tenure. Furthermore, it set a standard—the bar, as it were. If others around you made partner within a reasonably similar number of years, that's the benchmark where things naturally kick in. If 10 years was the standard, the very thought of someone making partner in, say, seven, was utterly outlandish.

Discussion concerning this issue revolved around two perspectives. One was that we needed more leaders and we needed them to develop faster. We simply could not have exponential growth unless we grew our people faster and more responsively. On the other hand, particularly with regard to people with a significant amount of years to their credit, a lot of other people were simply going to track faster. That made career trajectory, one largely based on longevity of service, completely irrelevant. That kind of seniority was done and out the door.

Instead, once again, it was an emphasis on results. Who's getting the job done? Although that understandably ruffled some feathers, it also made all the sense in the world. A simple comparison made the argument. Consider one person with 10 years of middling performance with another's seven years characterized by consistently outstanding work. Who better to move ahead first?

Furthermore, it was about promoting greater control over your own career track. When we would speak to prospective employees, we emphasized they have a significant influence over how quickly they progress. They should be able to influence that more than simply ticking off a scorecard of the number of years of service.

It was an enormous boost to our recruiting efforts, as well as our retention. If you worked at HORNE, the message was loud and clear: Here, you have the ability to own your career. If you wanted to grow your career, to move quickly if you wanted to move quickly, results were the ticket to that destination, not the tick of a clock. Whether it was a matter of attracting top talent or keeping them on board, it was a very big deal.

This did present us with what can only be described as a somewhat delicate challenge—situations where relatively young people were placed in positions supervising somewhat older colleagues. That meant better and particularly comprehensive leadership training earlier in people's careers. First was the challenge of showing a younger person just what constituted good leadership skills, such as leading by example and, while leading others, allowing them sufficient autonomy to do their work in the way they deemed most effective and best focused.

We also emphasized the significant value of emotional intelligence—including a capacity to empathize with others and to come to understand and appreciate their values and priorities.

Finally, and perhaps most important of all, younger leaders needed to recognize that the chances were very good that their older colleagues had experience in areas they might be unfamiliar with. They likely possessed skills the younger leader had yet to fully develop. These were the tools, skills, and knowledge that our younger leaders needed to acquire to be effective leaders—starting very early in their careers.

CAREER GROWTH CONTINUUMS AND INFORMATION EQUITY

Looking back at these and other powerful initiatives we introduced as we gathered momentum on our Wise Firm journey, it's interesting to observe how, taken as a group, they addressed two central elements to working at HORNE. On one hand, there was the emphasis on building a sense of belonging—the energy and focus that derives from a group of committed people coming together as one. On the other, there was the journey as it related to the individual. We also strove to develop and implement programs which would aid individual teammates in their career growth and career ownership—how to overcome challenges, work more effectively with others, and direct their professional energy in the most productive direction. It was the ideal complement to our focus on results and the individual's empowerment to drive their own career progress. If you wanted to move forward and were willing to produce the results to make that happen, we would provide you with every means possible to expedite your efforts.

That ultimately led to the creation of the career growth continuum. In a nutshell, the continuum focused on establishing clarity with regard to teammates' career expectations—a clearly delineated set of expected competencies and behaviors that determined how teammates could move forward in their HORNE careers.

This, like other initiatives, circled back to two established hurdles. One was simply that some teammates had access to certain types of information and guidance that others did not. And, partly as a result, promotions and career movement were frequently inequitable. In effect, people were being promoted for a variety of different and often confusing reasons.

The career growth continuum was put in place specifically to address those sorts of issues. Honed and refined over time, the continuum helped lay out guidelines to help teammates understand valuable core competencies, not merely technical skills. From there, the continuum specified how these attributes applied to every level throughout the firm, all the way up to senior manager. There was even a continuum for partners based on those exact same core attributes.

We wanted people to know that they had ownership of their career but that they weren't in it by themselves. We would set out very clear and equitable expectations, we were going to give them the resources for them to own in their development, and we were going to train—for lack of a better term—the behaviors that we would reward and that we believed would help them be successful.

Furthermore, there was greater equity of information. Not only did that level the playing field, but it also resulted in better career movement decisions. People were moving ahead because of what they could do rather than simply knowing something that others weren't aware of.

The program helped clarify career growth across the spectrum at HORNE. We could stand in front of newly hired teammates and discuss in detail the core areas by which they would be evaluated and progress in their HORNE careers—the very same parameters by which the highest-positioned people in the firm were also measured. All of this was driven by results for growing our people and other leaders, as well as growing our firm, with exceptional client service.

By coincidence, these core areas included lots of soft skills that are now so desperately needed in the marketplace to be successful. When you commit to a people-first culture, people skills immediately become important and impact the ability of someone to advance in their careers. Of course, we don't call them *soft* skills at HORNE. They're *success* skills.

The continuum also created clarity of expectations. It allowed us to have accountability discussions that were more concrete and empirical. It gave our managers a clear game plan. Most of all, it led to better conversations within our firm. As a result, our people skills grew enormously. This increased our effectiveness in establishing a strong sense of belonging and providing a *wow!* client experience.

I don't know how many hours of conversation we had about the career growth continuum and those areas they needed to address to progress in their careers. In effect, for those in leadership positions looking to help others progress, we emphasized that every team member needed growth and development in the key areas of people development, client experience, firm growth, leadership, and Wise Firm culture. But it wasn't a matter of simply excelling at one aspect of the continuum and you're bound for a promotion. It was the commitment to equip and develop leaders faster and with better conversations and clarity on how to be successful at HORNE.

This was yet another significant game changer. And, naturally enough, there was some discomfort. There were those who genuinely wanted a check-the-box methodology—cover all these things on the checklist, and then you can become a supervisor. But we wanted more than a rudimentary laundry list.

The tool proved invaluable in helping team members start to see their own paths. In effect, it encouraged people toward greater self-evaluation, looking to identify on their own what attributes needed to be strengthened and what professional weaknesses needed to be addressed. It was a game changer in how we grew and developed people. It effectively reinvented our performance management processes. It changed how we evaluated all team members.

Our mindset shifted from qualifications to getting people experiences that helped them grow and learn. We shifted to promoting quickly for faster growth. We all learn as we assume larger roles, and people are ready for the next challenge much sooner than we usually allow. Years of experience and time sheets showing high utilization do not define potential or the value of actual results.

From a more global standpoint, the career growth continuum effectively rebuilt our entire learning and development process. As a result, every element of our skill-building initiatives was focused on the leadership success skills teammates truly needed to make a difference. Looked at another way, as we were moving toward clarity for what we were trying to be at HORNE, we also stressed the skills that supported and complemented that.

As is necessary for real culture transformation, the career growth continuum had its internal champions. Former HORNE team member Ashley McAdams deserves a great deal of credit for first envisioning the need to address gaps in our feedback skills. And, once again, former teammate Kassi Rushing was instrumental in putting those ideas into actual practice—proof positive once more of the need for proactive, engaged role models to move a culture in the best direction possible.

This is a reminder that one leader alone or even a small group of leaders can't successfully navigate a journey from good to great. It takes team members from every area of the firm to embrace the vision early and begin to drive the change on a conversation-by-conversation basis. Early adopters who celebrate progress and demonstrate embracing the new direction are critical to building momentum. Trusting and transparent leaders who consistently demonstrate these values with their actions determine how fast you can go. The leadership fishbowl is always on display for the team.

THE LOWEST MOMENT

"This too shall pass." That expression, a favorite saying of my father-in-law, James Cole, lovingly called Poppy, echoed in my head as we continued in our effort to build the Wise Firm.

So far on our journey, it always seemed to be two steps forward and then a step back. Every time we seemed to be making progress, we would find ourselves with another challenge. Still, nothing could have prepared us for the two-by-four that landed squarely in our face. It was the one time that I thought the swamp might defeat us, that our journey would fall short, that God had another purpose in mind. Did I misunderstand God's vision? All I really knew at this point was a crippling insecurity about our journey. It was the lowest of low points and no doubt the most stressful time in my 38-year career.

We were invested heavily in our future view. Using our anticipatory mindset—a building block of the Wise Firm and a strategy and skill set we fine-tuned with the wisdom and guidance from Daniel Burrus, author of *The Anticipatory Organization*.[11]

Technology-driven change is accelerating at an exponential rate and will continue for the foreseeable future. This means there is and will be digital transformation that results in those who are disrupted and those who are the disruptor. Burrus helps you understand how to separate the hard trends, which *will* happen, from the soft trends, which *might* happen, allowing you to jump ahead with low risk and provide the confidence that comes from certainty. By anticipating the opportunities from hard and soft

---

11 Daniel Burrus, *The Anticipatory Organization: Turn Disruption and Change Into Opportunity and Advantage* (Greenleaf Book Group Press, 2017).

trends, we began to strategically place our firm, our services, and our skills to help shape our future by helping our team members and clients capture some of these future opportunities. For our business model, we grew our anticipatory skills to be distinctive in who we were as a firm and how we served clients.

Anticipating the technology disruption and accelerating digital transformation for the next 10 years, from 2016 to 2018, we invested millions in IT development, including migration to a new document management system, and implemented and elevated our infrastructure, including new and better tools for remote working, while developing three comprehensive client software solutions. We were all in, not just with our vision for exponential growth but for our commitment to remote workforce and significant investment with our wallets. We were way beyond putting our toes in the water, more like a head-first dive.

However, in 2018, for the first time in our journey, we lost out on not one but *four* very large, multiyear projects. Something went awry on each one. Losing all four really stung; winning even just one of these projects would have had a huge impact on our growth and profitability. Compounding our disappointment was the fact that our custom IT development was designated for two of these lost projects. We simply had nowhere to deploy it. Some might call it bad luck or horrible timing, but in the end, we must own our outcomes. We executed poorly, and our collaboration and creativity were not our best by a country mile. The truth is, we simply got shut out.

Cumulatively, the losses were a game changer (*game stopper* might be the more appropriate term). By this point, we had incurred significant long- and short-term debt, which dwarfed any amount of debt in our history. We had a strong lineup of team members who were all-in for building the Wise Firm—and frankly, some of the best in our profession. We simply could not cut into the muscle, meaning we couldn't trim overhead by reducing headcount, because that headcount was the very thing that would set us apart from others as we went forward. We looked up, and we were in the middle of the swamp—dark, deep, and scary.

I was wracked with my own misgivings. Was this what we really should have been doing the whole time? Was this the right path? Why wasn't God blessing our journey as He faithfully had so far?

During those few months in late 2018 and early 2019, it was very common for me to wake up at 3:00 a.m. consumed by stress and wondering what direction we needed to go. What were we doing wrong? I knew I was not alone in losing sleep. The board—as well as some partners and directors, I'm sure—recognized this could threaten our ability to remain an independent firm. We could see how dire the situation had become. We entered 2019 knowing we needed to turn this bad streak around.

But then came yet another convergence of God, faith, and culture. In my experience, God never lets a crisis go to waste. He always has a way of using them to put us back on track and further His greater purpose. What a coincidence for us to experience this incredibly bad losing streak at a time when we had our largest debt leverage ever and had made our biggest investments in people, technology, and resources.

I know God used this time to put me on my knees and to look to Him, rather than grabbing the steering wheel as I had been attempting to do. (When you think about it, we never really *do* have the steering wheel.) I knew in my heart and soul that we had been genuinely pursuing God's plan for our firm, that we were trying to honor Him with our service to others. Still, I had become blind to how little I was really surrendering to God. We had experienced significant success up until this point in our journey, and success brings an illusion of competency and self-sufficiency that is unhealthy, if not simply dangerous. I was obviously bathing in it.

I can't speak for others, but I know God used this crisis to teach me the power of turning completely to His will and relying on Him—true surrender. Frankly, I was letting the fear of failure define my focus. This smothering fear, this doubt, this unknown future was driving out the joy that God was providing in our daily journey. I literally prayed daily, asking God to lead us and show us the way forward. On His own timetable, God taught me to leave my fears at His feet.

As I surrendered my fears and worries to God, I focused on these two scriptures as we fought off the paralyzing effect of fear:

"For I know the plans I have for you, declares the Lord, plans to prosper you and not to harm you, plans to give you hope and a future."

—JEREMIAH 29:11 NIV

"Being confident in this that He who began a good work in you will carry it on to completion until the day of Jesus Christ."

—PHILIPPIANS 1:6 NIV

It's simply a different journey when you trust God and look to serve others and honor Him. He helped me confidently communicate with our partner group where we were as a firm, emphasizing our renewed and continued commitment to our plan and strategy.

Together, we would overcome this. In that group conversation, I asked each partner to not only pray but also to stay diligent in leveraging every opportunity. We were positioned almost perfectly, but we had to execute. My notes from that meeting remind me that I shared the confidence that God had given me. "I will not blink. God has His hands on our firm, and we will make it through this challenge and continue to thrive in building the Wise Firm together."

Shortly after this, in early 2019, we won a huge project. We were off to the races as we began to collaborate and execute on numerous opportunities that "by coincidence" kept coming our way. For all that I had wrestled with concerning what I could do myself, God taught me that everything would happen on His timeline. He asked me to trust Him, and that's exactly what I started doing.

Taking everything together, we had not only weathered the challenges and uncertainty that had hindered us only a short time before, but we had many of the mindsets and practical aspects of the Wise Firm in place. The journey of the Wise Firm was under full sail. The results began to speak for themselves.

|||||||||||||||||||||||||||||||||||||||||||||||||||||||||||||||||||||||||||||||||||||||||||||||||||||||||||||||||||||||||||

MAGNETIC THOUGHTS

"As iron sharpens iron, so one person sharpens another."

—PROVERBS 27:17 NIV

"A generous person will prosper;
whoever refreshes others will be refreshed."

—PROVERBS 11:25 NIV

- The journey to a magnetic culture will have some very low points and painful experiences. It takes uncommon courage, fanatical discipline, and a group of committed leaders to stay the course.

- Resistance always comes with the initiative of change. It's simply how we are wired. Understand what the why might be behind the resistance, as you will not only need the early adopters but the conversion of many of these initial resistors.

- In my experience, changing a person's mindset by simply directing or demanding that it change is a fool's errand. Culture change happens only when people choose to join in, and the way to open the door for mindset shifts is to offer sufficient information and insights while continuing to invite them along. Observing celebrations of success or the fear of being left out are two powerful drivers for those who, for whatever reason, lag behind.

- The legacy question *Are we moving too fast?* should be flipped and replaced with the more relevant question: *Are we moving fast enough?* We do not live in a world of incremental change; the status quo is one of the riskiest decisions we can make.

- Full potential coaches—integrated within the team full time as part of people development have been game changers for us. Unlike sponsorships, coaching helps team members develop their own skills, learn tools to help them excel in their work, and operate in complete confidentiality. Coaching demonstrates people-first mindset.

- Going from good to great meant always having enough great team members. To ensure this, we turned to excess staffing and increased our target for recruiting to be 10 percent above our expected need. This cost more in the short run, but it positioned us to take on larger projects, grow faster, and innovate more. It was anticipatory of the talent war we saw on the horizon. More powerfully, it let us ask, *What's possible?*

- Because we were so focused on results, we changed the way we promoted. Why wait for an annual review? If someone knocks it out of the park in October, they should be promoted in October. We also threw seniority out the window. These approaches were enormous boosts to our recruiting efforts, as well as our retention of great talent.

- We shifted our mindset from qualifications to getting people experiences, promoting quickly for faster growth. Neither years of experience nor time sheets define potential.

- Teaching different generations of team members and leaders the value of collaborating for results is critical for exponential growth.

- We put in place a career growth continuum to lay out guidelines for promotion—including not just technical skills but also core competencies (soft skills). This helped align expectations among managers and led to even greater self-development among team members.

- God never lets a crisis go to waste. When our firm hit a major low, I did what I should have been doing more: turned wholeheartedly to God and prayed for direction.

||||||||||||||||||||||||||||||||||||||||||||||||||||||||||||||||||||||||||||||||||||||||||||||||||||||

8

Coincidences, Magnetic Energy, and the Chance to Play Again Tomorrow

COINCIDENCES—THEY JUST KEEP COMING, one right after the other. Having six chapters of this book drafted by mid-December 2021, I was so looking forward to the last two weeks of the year, where I could disconnect from the firm and the book to enjoy some downtime at our camp near Eagle Lake in Mississippi. Every year, I use this time to recharge, spend quality time with family, and enjoy God's creation, whether that's hunting or fishing.

It was December 17, and the temperatures had been unseasonably warm. Whenever it warms up, I think fishing first. Having had two successful trips the prior week to Eagle Lake to catch some beautiful crappie, I decided to fish again rather than hunt.

After three hours, I hadn't landed a single fish. It was 3:30 p.m. I figured if I loaded my boat and rushed back to camp, I could actually be on stand 12 with a favorable wind by 4:15. Slipping on a jacket and keeping my fishing shoes on, I arrived at the stand at 4:20. Although I was excited to get some hunting in, I knew my chances weren't particularly good; it was my first hunt of the year, and I had yet to scout the area.

Still, only 10 minutes later, a program buck (a mature buck large enough to harvest by the club rules) running a doe passed within 50 yards. I decided to pass as well. At 4:45, another big eight-point buck came out of the thicket about 75 yards away. What unbelievable luck! But I decided to pass on that one as well, as he was similar to other eight points that I'd taken over the last 18 years.

By now, it was 4:55 and getting close to dark. Another big buck came out of the same thicket. I immediately put my binoculars down, as all I could see were horns going everywhere. This was an absolute monster. He turned broadside at 75 yards, walking very slowly. As I raised my rifle, I was trembling. Thankfully, I harvested him on the first and only shot—a beautiful 13 point, weighing a whopping 230 pounds. (For fact checkers and skeptics, you can go to my Instagram and see a picture of this beautiful trophy.)

Now to the coincidence: Earlier in this book, I shared the story of harvesting the largest deer ever at my friend and partner Dee Boykin's hunting club. That took place on January 15, 2011. I harvested this second buck almost 10 years later to the day. The first one happened in the morning, the second in the waning light of late afternoon. The first occurred just as I was beginning my journey toward becoming managing partner; the second took place at the end of my tenure as managing partner.

In a sense, those two bucks serve as bookends of my tenure as the company's managing partner. But it's important to understand that those two bucks were far from everyday harvests. Trophy deer (club records in both cases) like these are truly rare. It's like winning the lottery not once but twice. Coincidences? Hardly.

By now, I'm certain you realize my description of coincidence after coincidence is very tongue in cheek. God's hand has been on all of them. Throughout our journey toward the Wise Firm, God has repeatedly blessed us and touched so many lives in so many remarkable ways. They simply just keep coming—even as I am writing this book!

As the journey that followed showed, God rarely shows His plans or timeline. Rather, He leads us one day at a time—just so far as we have faith and are willing to ask.

WAS IT WORTH IT? DID IT WORK? A CHECKLIST

At this point in the narrative, it's natural to wonder whether all the challenges, struggles, laughter, and tears that embodied our pilgrimage toward the Wise Firm were really worth it. To address that question, here's a quick checklist of some of our major objectives:

- Magnetic energy? You can feel it everywhere!

- A stronger sense of belonging—more than 90 percent? Absolutely!

- Flexibility? Indeed! Unrivaled—and thank goodness!

- Reduced turnover? Significantly better!

- Retention of star teammates? Again, significantly better!

- Expanded leadership? Absolutely!

- Faster leader development? Certainly, not to mention a broader application of what it means to develop as a leader.

- Leadership pipeline? Much improved!

- Improved client experience? Just ask them (that means yes)!

- Improved diversity and inclusion? Without a doubt! And all the way to ownership!

- Exponential growth? How does more than 500 percent in 10 years sound?

- Improved profitability? You bet!

- Improved relevance? Most certainly!

- Consistently serving a higher purpose? Spot on!

- Game over? Victory declared? Well . . .

That's where this checklist jumps the tracks. After all that effort and achievement, is the journey finished? Have you actually won? No and yes.

SUCCESS—CULTURE'S GREATEST ENEMY

First off, the no portion of the answer: When it comes to developing and nurturing magnetic culture, there simply is no end point. Culture is a living, breathing entity and, as such, can never be simply set aside to continue on its own. It needs ongoing attention and care. It's a pilgrimage whose destination effectively keeps moving forward, no matter how much progress you're able to achieve.

In fact, the reality of the never-ending journey can pose pitfalls for even the best-intentioned pilgrims. If, by chance, you feel you've finally arrived, you feel you've made it last—watch out. Not only are you not to your destination yet—and truly never will be—but the pride and satisfaction you derive from mistakenly thinking you've reached the end can compromise the entire journey. Once you stop treating it as a trip with no end and—in effect, put your feet up to relax—that's when the culture you've worked so hard to build can begin to deteriorate (much like, for instance, a bag of hamburger lost in the wheel well of a car that begins to rot).

In effect, success becomes the enemy of magnetic culture. As you build momentum and experience success, oddly enough, that success morphs into culture's greatest enemy. It curtails discipline to continue to work hard to win the next day. Success brings with its sweetness a buffet of temptations to shove you off course.

Remember the client service mantras we had echoing down our halls as we reflected on our "good" culture? Success is exceedingly good at breeding the infamous control vampires. These human vampires are simply wired to grab the steering wheel at every opportunity. They live for more control. The slide away from excellence begins when leaders start to elevate client service to being the number-one message across the firm, instead of keeping it on the people within the firm.

It's very common to hear the same rally cries from most hallways today. "Oh, there's a mistake in client service, so it's time to stress client service as our most important focus." (You'll hear that, even though all cultures will experience client failures—after all, humans tend to operate that way.)

Maybe this rally cry captures it better: "It's all about client service;

otherwise, we don't exist!" That's tough to argue with because, at face value, it's a true statement. However, it's just part of the puzzle. How do we deliver amazing client service consistently and in the long run? How do we make this who we are?

Here, my favorite Mark Twain quote proves superbly relevant: "It's not what we don't know that gets us in trouble; it's what we know for sure that just ain't so!"

It's too easy for leaders to quickly forget what really elevates client service to a *wow!* experience, what delivers a more consistent experience, and what leads to exponential growth in the first place. As control vampires jump on the first client service failure to grab back turf—that, or success has clouded their vision of where the magnetic energy came from—the focus shifts to a short-term obsession with success rather than significance in people's lives. That dilutes culture and, in the long run, client service.

BEEN THERE, DONE THAT

When we experience growth and success, we all have a natural tendency to relax. We start believing more in our genius and creativity and fail to realize it is the magnetic energy of the people, the team's sense of belonging and caring, and the team's genius and beBetter mindset that generate high performance and consistently amazing client experiences. Magnetic energy attracts and retains talent, filling up a leadership pipeline that supports amazing client service and exponential growth.

We are often so quick to grab that steering wheel and forget it's God who has blessed us as we are serving others and honoring Him. We (especially me) certainly drifted away from our intentional focus on collaboration and the power of we. It can become a slippery slope as leaders shift focus to client service first and foremost.

Then, the inevitable happens: Client service stumbles or the loss of valuable talent hits hard. That's when the blame game can shift into overdrive. Trust erodes, magnetic energy drains away, and leaders are hesitant to look at where the team lost touch with great culture and high performance. This is often followed with reams of rules and processes to "guarantee" client-first delivery.

This is completely misdirected. As failures increase and mediocrity blooms, the real cause is team members not trusting leadership or each other. As a result, discretionary efforts that generate high performance decline. And it all starts as we begin to feel good about our success and forget the uncommon discipline that empowered people to make it happen in the first place.

If you find your team on this fast track to mediocrity, think about what really drove magnetic energy and growth. The sooner that's done, the easier it is to find sound footing. By embracing the mindset of people first, you can step away from the blame game, bravely look at what changed, and reconnect to people as priority. Remember that magnetic culture is a mindset, a daily journey that requires courage and uncommon discipline.

MAGNETIC CULTURE IS A DAILY COMMITMENT

Now to the yes portion of the answer to balance things out. Nurturing the development of magnetic culture doesn't have an end point, a finish line where you've arrived. All you can hope for is that, by pursuing that goal with energy and commitment, you earn the right to play another day.

But that's wonderful—for many reasons.

For one thing, it represents another step forward. You can see daily progress, continual movement toward your objective. It's energizing and boosts your resolve to keep at the battle.

Moreover, you don't start the next day in the same position you were yesterday or even a week prior. You're stronger. Your commitment has grown. Perhaps teammates whose resolve might have been shaky can see the progress themselves and, as a result, find their own commitment growing as well. As a group, you start the day with a lead that continues to grow as the days pass. The rope that everyone is pulling begins to move more easily!

Frankly, the magnetic energy also begins to pull you along, and with the rising trust, everything begins to move faster—particularly learning. Learn fast, learn forward, learn together. Isn't that what many of us are struggling with, teams that can't learn and move fast enough?

Building your community, your tribe, and your people and contributing to something bigger than yourself provide those people with meaning and purpose. Why we work impacts directly how we work. The resulting significance in people's lives drives joy and fulfillment.

Those outside your team—your clients and your community—can also see it for themselves. Ironically, by reemphasizing people and culture every single day, the goal of client first—the windmills so many companies mistakenly charge—is strengthened.

Perhaps most valuable of all, recognizing that the battle to achieve magnetic culture is a daily one that never ends, you can skirt the false security of success. You don't become complacent; you never let down your energy and resolution. You never forget to reinforce the message that the journey is hard but that it's essential to stay the course. Things may indeed get worse before they get better, but the pain will be worth it.

You continue to emphasize the essential importance of open, transparent communication and the necessity of having candid and frequently difficult conversations. But you keep having them, one conversation at a time.

You also understand that yours is a somewhat singular journey. Building a magnetic culture doesn't happen with a paint-by-numbers approach. What works in one setting may be utterly useless elsewhere. By taking on the battle on a daily basis, you come to recognize what genuinely works for you—and you reapply it, day in and day out. Your commitment is bolstered with flexibility.

Just as important is the recognition of what my friend Dan Burrus calls a "hard trend"—those trends that are absolutely certain to take place. The world doesn't stay the way it was. People and technology are changing at warp speed. Even the so-called status quo creeps and crawls until it falls off the edge all at once.

That's the case with culture. Even good culture starts to stink the longer it says the same. That's particularly true today. With constant change all around us, good culture will spoil much sooner than in the past. It's critical to start your journey now, embrace brutal reality—whatever it is—and take action. Consider the power of contrasting the old with the new, who you are versus who you want to be, as we did with the initial Wise Firm building blocks.

Culture doesn't change because someone appoints a task force, pins up a brochure on a bulletin board, hires a diversity officer, or signs a pledge. That last one always grates on me. What an easy out—just sign here because we know the journey is too difficult to make a real difference. A signature's good enough.

Culture changes when someone decides that the way things are around here need to change. The status quo is not enough. Good culture will not take us where we need to go. You must simply have the courage to begin to communicate a compelling vision and back it up by doing things differently—one conversation at a time, until someone else picks up the rope and pulls along with you. It might help to also remember that unity does not mean uniformity. Diverse teams with a strong sense of belonging win the long game every time. The journey starts only if we grab hold first and do not let go.

MAGNETIC ENERGY

Magnetic culture and high performance only evolve from workplaces where people feel loved and cared for—workplaces where they have a strong sense of belonging and are appreciated for who they are and what strengths they bring to the team, workplaces where they are building something bigger than themselves.

That sort of workplace fuels discretionary effort to reach every teammate's full potential. That, in turn, fosters magnetic energy. At the end of a hard day or a long week, teammates are fulfilled because they can see and feel the impact of their individual contributions. Their energy is magnified as they have helped others with their sense of belonging and elevated their performance.

Taken together, this collaboration, trust, and discretionary effort are a combined force that is distinctive, magnetic, and transformative for any culture. As teams build trust, as it grows further into unconditional trust, it fuels world-class performance and client experiences. This is magnetic energy. It makes a difference in our journey every day.

Intentional culture is more than beliefs and behaviors. It's the magnetic energy that attracts talent and leads to discretionary effort behind high performance. It's the common values that provide a true north for a ship under full sail. It's the tribe, the sense of belonging that we all search for, something bigger than ourselves. It's the compelling vision of what we are building together. It's the flexibility to do life empowered. People choose to bring meaning, purpose, effort, and belief to work.

Pursuing great culture and high performance takes an enormous amount of courage. It requires courage and uncommon discipline to consistently make people more important than short-term profits, to put people before control, to put people before power. It takes courage and uncommon discipline to align actions with words and vision. As I reiterated earlier, there is nothing in this daily journey that is easy. It is hard, and yet it is worth it in every respect—from fulfillment, joy, and growth to long-term relevance and profitability.

Negative energy can stall innovation. It's understandable. It takes courage and uncommon discipline to pursue magnetic energy because humans are humans. We are complex, messy, and imperfect. Speaking just for myself, this journey put a spotlight on my shortcomings on a daily basis. Every great culture will suffer mistakes, people failures, and client service failures. Remember there is no such thing as a perfect culture.

The journey is hard because you do not have all the answers, people are volatile and complicated, you have limited control, and you're prioritizing things that are contrary to the common short-term focus promoted by business as usual. You don't have established measuring sticks, and not everything can be connected directly to the bottom line or growth. You are measuring things that have never been measured. It takes some faith to continue to believe in people and the process of empowerment. It's hard because we want to take it and squeeze it so we feel in control. But that's exactly what squeezes the magnetic energy out of culture. On the other hand, leadership and magnetic energy will help pull the team forward.

By the way, magnetic culture is nothing about being soft or less accountable. Oddly, the opposite is true as you gain momentum. Mediocrity sticks out, complacency stinks, and the sounds of resistance hurt everyone's ears. People actually ask for more clarity, take more ownership in goals and results, and overall goal setting elevates. It's actually the norm to have high expectations. In our particular journey, we built more accountability at every stage. Great cultures have and promote high expectations with the joy of people pursuing their full potential together.

As the proverb says, "If you want to go fast, go alone. If you want to go far, go together." Magnetic cultures go together. We before me. One team, one direction. And magnetic energy fuels that journey!

GREAT LEADERSHIP IS NOT A SINGLE LEADER

That proverb is particularly applicable to our journey at HORNE. Whether you are starting your journey from good culture to great or trying to keep a culture great as you experience success, it is never about one person. It takes a group of leaders who share beliefs, a compelling vision, and the commitment that change is needed, that the future depends on putting people first.

Magnetic culture comes from great leadership provided by people who are willing to not only stand together but to push forward as one. They support and strengthen each other. Leaders demonstrate they care and consistently extend trust to people. Courage and confidence build as you make progress. People see the courage and commitment to be different and grow in courage and commitment.

Our journey has been blessed at every turn with so many leaders, so many champions, so many team members who were early adopters and who made a difference every day with uncommon discipline and courage.

What did I learn from these leaders and so many other up-and-coming stars during our journey? The easy thing to see is that we are human and made more mistakes than we care to count. As a group, we learned from those mistakes and found ways to grow as a leadership team. We stayed strong through these mistakes (many of them mine) by giving each other the benefit of good intentions.

Our leaders demonstrated courage and transparency by living the vision. They were authentic in how they each led and communicated our future vision. They were coachable and learned new skills and expertise. They took this knowledge and experience and became daily coaches for our team members. They connected with teams and individuals as they helped us implement our people-first practices and behaviors. Conversation by conversation and collaboration by collaboration, they worked to understand how we could be better. They listened to our team members to ensure every voice counted. Those are lessons I'll never stop embracing.

During our setbacks, they would not let us drop our heads. They never failed to encourage each other and our team members. Over and over, they reminded us what, in fact, it meant to be us. With their guidance, we found a rhythm—one conversation at a time, communications repeated over and over and then again in all those one-on-one conversations.

Samir El Hage is a special story; he demonstrated vision, trust, and courage as he merged into our firm in 2019 and helped plant our HORNE flag in Puerto Rico. Magnetic cultures grow and provide opportunities to expand, which sometimes means merging in other team members and leaders. Doing the due diligence to protect your culture and to establish a common vision is critical to success. Beware of mergers and acquisitions just for the sake of growth; a common vision of people first should always be front and center.

You need visionaries and early adopters from top leadership who champion embracing your brutal reality, challenge the status quo, lay out a plan to beBetter, and step forward together with vulnerability and trust.

Transitions of leadership can be very dicey—to say the least—for professional service firms. However, when you have magnetic energy, a magnetic culture, there will be leaders ready and willing to lead. Magnetic cultures grow leaders faster, and their in-built trust allows everyone to embrace a mindset of abundance rather than scarcity and competition. Again, we were blessed with so many leaders who stepped up in various roles to elevate our journey. They came to fight for a better and brighter future every day.

Their commitment and leadership reminded me so much of the great speech popularly known as "The Man in the Arena," given by Theodore Roosevelt in 1910.[12] This is my *modern-day* version of his speech:

> *It is not the critic who counts; not the person who points out how the strong person stumbles, or where the doer of deeds could have done them better. The credit belongs to the person who is actually in the arena, whose face is marred by dust and sweat and blood; who strives valiantly; who errs, who comes short again and again, because there is no effort without error and shortcoming; but who does actually strive to do the deeds; who knows great enthusiasms, the great devotions; who spends themselves in a worthy cause; who at the best knows in the end the triumph of high achievement, and who at the worst, if they fail, at least fails while daring greatly, so that their place shall never be with those cold and timid souls who neither know victory nor defeat.*

We actually had a leader recite this quote to us at our annual partner meeting in July 2020. We wanted to celebrate and recognize that the journey we chose, the vision to build a magnetic, people-first culture was

---

12 Theodore Roosevelt, "Citizenship in a Republic," speech at the Sorbonne, Paris, France, April 23, 1910, https://www.theodorerooseveltcenter.org/Learn-About-TR/TR-Encyclopedia/Culture-and-Society/Man-in-the-Arena.aspx.

not easy, and that each of us should celebrate and recognize each other for being one of those in the arena. For magnetic culture, you *must* dare greatly, strive valiantly, commit to a compelling vision, seek full potential, expect high performance, and care about others. You are recognizing the good in people. Believe and trust in the good!

LEADERSHIP, KNOWLEDGE, WISDOM, AND EXPERIENCE FROM OUTSIDE

We also benefited so much from so many leaders outside of our team. To truly grow a magnetic culture with high performance, you need influence from dynamic leaders outside of your core teams, as well as beyond your profession. You need the experience, insights, support, and challenges from champions who are leading with a positive future view outside of what is your usual sphere of interaction.

Our journey has been blessed with so many great influencers who have not only shared their knowledge but have become cheerleaders for our team. They've shown up to make a difference. Our firm is better for knowing them as both advisors and friends. Although we were blessed with many, there were five who not only shared their insights, experience, and wisdom but came alongside us in our journey with love, support, and friendship.

Sam Allred, from Upstream Academy, is the architect with Hugh Parker of our partner performance review process, which elevated accountability with a strong people-development and leadership focus. His partner, Tim Bartz, was the visionary who led us in 2011 as we changed our business model. As he defined visioneering, our eyes opened so we could think bigger and bolder.

John O'Leary really inspired us to continue our journey to beBetter, to love and care. John's book, *On Fire*, is a favorite of the HORNE team, and it was so impactful on me that I gave copies to all of our kids, my parents, and several friends.

Tom Hood, who serves as executive vice president of the American Institute of Certified Public Accountants, is one of the most influential people in public accounting and a member of the Top 30 Thought Leaders. He brought a wealth of insights and future-view perspectives and led several of our strategic planning retreats. Tom is always checking in to see how we are doing.

Futurist Daniel Burrus helped change our way of thinking. As our culture got stronger and we worked more on making our client experience distinctive, developing the skill set of being anticipatory was a game changer. I cannot say enough how much Dan impacted our future view, and he has continued to provide help and support along the way.

Our journey has been impacted so much by the wisdom and sharing of strategies by many leaders in our profession who became fast friends, as well as mentors and advisors. You can find members of my personal board of directors in my acknowledgments.

The point is that, as you build a professional network of leaders, their wisdom and creative ideas can help you avoid the proverbial swamp—or at least wallow in it less. Look to leaders outside of your company to help you better navigate the swamp that otherwise might swallow you. In our case, accessing these leaders helped us fast-track so many challenges and provided a launching pad for developing our future view. Make sure you hang out with smart people!

MAGNETIC THOUGHTS

"For lack of guidance a nation falls,
but victory is won through many advisors."

—PROVERBS 11:14 NIV

"Plans fail for lack of counsel, but with many advisors they succeed."

—PROVERBS 15:22 NIV

- Take coincidences with a large grain of salt. Remember that God leads us all, one day at a time. We just have to pay attention.

- Building magnetic energy never has an end point. All you can do is apply yourself by being intentional and demonstrating the commitment to win the day—and, from there, the right to play again the next day.

- Success is magnetic culture's second greatest enemy. (Only so-called good culture is more destructive.) Too often, the pride and satisfaction we derive from success diverts our attention from where the real magic is: *people.*

- Success can also trick us into thinking we have arrived. We never arrive and must be intentional every day.

- Too many firms think putting customers first will solve their problems; the reality is, if you put your own people first, customer service will elevate.

- Culture doesn't change because someone appoints a task force, pins up a brochure on a bulletin board, hires a diversity officer, or signs a pledge. It changes when someone decides it's time to do the hard work and has the courage to communicate a compelling vision and back it up by doing things differently.

- Magnetic culture evolves from a group of leaders sharing a vision and extending trust. You are recognizing the good in people. Believe and trust in the good! No one leader can do it alone.

- Pursuing great culture and high performance requires courage and discipline. It requires aligning actions with words and vision and putting people first.

- "If you want to go fast, go alone. If you want to go far, go together." Magnetic cultures go together. It's we before me.

- Magnetic cultures grow leaders faster. Trust them, and get out of the way.

- Do not chase growth for the sake of growth. Bigger is not necessarily better. Stay true to your people-first vision.

- To truly grow a magnetic culture with high performance, you need influence from dynamic leaders outside of your core teams and beyond your profession. You need the experience, insights, support, and challenges from champions who are leading with the view of a positive future.

More Coincidences
and Final Thoughts

I'VE REPEATEDLY REFERRED TO THE so-called coincidences that have characterized HORNE's ongoing journey to build the Wise Firm. To wrap up this book, here's one coincidence we need to pay close attention to. People are intentionally looking for workplaces that provide significance to their lives. They are searching for inspiration, purpose, and the ability to make a difference. They want to know what they do has significance and helps others. They are desperate to belong to a community, a tribe, a cause where they can be their best and again be significant. By coincidence, the core of this book is about how everyone can intentionally lead with significance.

People are going to continue to walk away—or, even worse, stay and be totally disengaged—if we don't wake up to the destructive path of workplaces that are clinging to "good" culture. As Arianna Huffington said, it's the Great Reevaluation. A recent survey of over 3,000 US workers showed that 38 percent don't trust their team members.[13] Pizza days,

---

13 "Why Community Matters in the New World of Work," BetterUp Insights Report 2022, BetterUp, 2022, https://grow.betterup.com/resources/build-a-culture-of-connection-report.

floating holidays, health initiatives, bring-a-pet—the list goes on fad after fad—and even raises are all nice. They really are; they can enhance a person's experience or create entitlement. It depends on the unique situation; you be the judge. One thing is for sure, they aren't the roots to creating magnetic culture. They don't bring meaning to work. They don't bring significance to a person's work, to their contribution, or to their life. They don't build a community or tribe, nor the commitment where people freely give discretionary efforts. We are missing the mark simply because this direction does not start and end by prioritizing a people-first mindset and strategy.

At a recent open discussion at a meeting of thought leaders in our profession, the issue of culture bubbled to the top almost immediately. The participants consistently mentioned how companies were failing to deliver purpose and meaning and to foster a genuine level of commitment and a sense of belonging. That really opened my eyes to how hungry people are to move forward and reinvent how they live and work. It's no longer just an issue of pay and benefits, but of meaning—a genuine, shared mindset of being valued and an integral part of something far greater than the individual. This hunger for meaning and significance is rampant across the business world.

HARD TO CHANGE

So why is it so hard to change when the evidence is so clear? Everyone has their reasons, excuses, challenges, and false beliefs and assumptions. Frankly, it's a long list; otherwise, we would see more companies with a magnetic, people-first culture. What have we learned in the journey of the Wise Firm that makes it hard?

- Good culture might get us by for a time, so it's not urgent.

- It takes courage and discipline to face our current reality.

- Changing priorities in strategic planning is hard to do.

- It takes faith that the numbers will be there even if we don't prioritize them.

- Stop measuring things that hold us back or some of our legacy KPIs.

- Start measuring things that haven't been measured before.

- We don't have a direct connection from improvement in culture to the bottom line.

- "Every voice counts" disrupts our hierarchy.

- Legacy success pulls at our souls.

- Extending trust makes us vulnerable.

- We love control of anything.

- Transparency is painful, especially when it's about what we need to improve.

- Seniority has been highly valued.

- Seeing is believing, and we are not consistent in our behaviors.

- We have toxic team members that do great work.

- Add-ons and fads are easier to implement and get lots of good press.

- Communicating with clarity and repeating it over and over gets old, even aggravating.

- More training costs resources.

- Proper onboarding slows down people being productive.

- Power is enticing.

- Growing others takes time and commitment.

- Coaches and coaching programs are expensive.

- People can find their own way.

- We don't like constructive feedback.

- We like being nice, so candor is hard.

- Full potential requires constant learning; we know enough.

- Feedback is painful. It takes a long time to really change culture.

- No time for one conversation at a time.

- Flexibility is not that important to our future.

- We have flexibility.

- People already know we care.

- I didn't need any of this when I started my career.

- Our stars are committed and will stay with us regardless.

- People know how well we do so they will stick to the course.

- This is a short-term cycle, and the leverage will shift back to the company.

- I'm just one person.

I'm sure by now you have already thought of several other reasons this is too hard or powerful excuses why you might not need or want to change course from the status quo. This prevalent status quo mindset threatens the relevance and viability of companies.

Culture is the most important and most powerful factor in business today. It is literally the soul of your organization. It should be the highest priority in every strategic plan. It should be measured and reported transparently to the entire team. As Peter Drucker says, "What gets measured, gets improved." I'm not sure who said culture eats strategy for breakfast, but today, culture will devour the entire future of your company if you don't prioritize it. It is far better to be a part of a magnetic culture growing people than a dying company clinging to control and only chasing more.

Think about this scenario: You can choose which team to join. Team one has a magnetic culture that underperformed on the top line last year. Team two has a "good" culture that struggles with turnover and loss of stars but sold more work than they ever have last year. Which team would present the best long-term career for you? Me, I'm going with team one every time, because they will solve the next challenge together. Team two will continue to burn out as they overwork their best and continue the slide to irrelevancy. Today the biggest challenge is not top-line growth, it's people growth.

EASY TO CHANGE

Why should this be an easy choice for each of us? Let's start with nobody likes the smelly hamburger trunk of the status quo.

- People actually want to be inspired.

- People want to beBetter.

- People want to be trusted.

- People love to work in high-trust teams.

- People love to be empowered to make choices on how to integrate careers and personal life.

- People love being part of something bigger than themselves.

- People like work with a purpose.

- People like high integrity in the organization and its leaders.

- People like consistency.

- People love positive energy.

- People like to be challenged.

- People love realizing their dreams.

- People like to be respected and appreciated.

- People love to know how they are contributing.

- People love living lives of significance.

- People experience inner joy when they are serving others.

- People love to have their voice heard.

- People love to share their creativity and ideas.

- People love to work for leaders who care about them.

- People like transparency.

- People love a sense of belonging.

If you got this far into the book, you already know plenty of other reasons this should be an easy choice for each of us.

THE CHOICE

Every day, your culture is either helping or hindering your purpose and mission. As individuals, every day we either strengthen our team's culture or weaken it. Faith-inspired values make a difference. Behaviors that honor those values build magnetic culture. Expectations and beliefs that support high trust and high performance will help create a strong sense of belonging. No culture is perfect, but that is not our goal. Our goal is to be on a daily journey of making our magnetic culture stronger with a beBetter mindset. Our goal isn't to make everyone happy. That's impossible too. We can have a workplace that's inclusive and purposeful, so people choose to be happy. We are choosing to recognize the good in people and trusting in it. Our goal is not to be a dream but to have a workplace where everyone can pursue their dreams. Everyone can help create a magnetic culture. Every voice counts. Everyone can be passionate about caring for others. Everyone can demonstrate a beBetter mindset. Everyone can help say no to what hurts our culture. Everyone can call out behaviors that have a negative impact on people. Everyone can be vulnerable and extend trust to others. Everyone can demonstrate bold leadership and take a stand. Everyone can help share the story. Everyone can be intentional to seek significance.

In life, we can make one of two choices. We can live a life of significance or a life chasing success. A life in pursuit of success is always driven by the thirst for more money, more power, more recognition, more promotions, more, more, more, and yet it's never enough. As much as we all wish to believe that there is, in fact, a finish line to it, there's no end or any real satisfaction. We may experience some fleeting happiness but no sustained joy. None of us will ever be declared the winner. In fact, some of the unhappiest people I have met in my lifetime have been very successful, wealthy people who spent their days chasing success in some manner as their top priority: a life focused on themselves.

That other path is a life of significance where we help build something bigger than ourselves, where people's lives are elevated and enhanced because we had an impact on them. A life where we can feel the lasting joy of serving others. A life of significance is one where we have pursued God's purpose for our lives, for our organization, rather than the fruits of our labor or profits. It has been eye opening for me. Once we began to focus on trusting, caring, and helping others, God simply blessed us with more: more people, more growth, more profits.

To flip this all around a bit, success actually follows significance. Significance, on the other hand, doesn't follow success. Magnetic culture allows people to pursue a life of significance while enjoying the success and blessings that come from working together and putting others first. I know God created us, and we are inherently imbued with the need to serve others and pursue building things bigger than ourselves. Magnetic culture is about a life of significance. We only get one life and one choice.

In a country so hungry to find work that matters and lives that have meaning, the courage to allow God, faith, and culture to converge shouldn't be a coincidence. Choose to beBetter. Pick up the rope, trust in the good in people, and champion that beautiful confluence.

Acknowledgments

SOMEONE RECENTLY ASKED ME, "JOEY, what would you change if you could go back in time?" It's a thought-provoking question, for certain. There are a million things I've gotten wrong, so on one hand, this could take a long time to answer. On the other hand, I am so thankful God chose to do so much with so little, and in my trust of His plan, I would not change a thing. Thank You, God, for all of Your blessings and for Your unending grace for my mistakes and shortcomings. I look back on all of God's coincidences and can now clearly see how He was using them to paint a story like this. I'm just grateful to be along for the ride.

My family loves me even during the many times that I am hard to love. Believe me, I can be really hard to love. Cathy, thanks for being beside me every step of the way. I appreciate and love you more every day. Rigby, Kelsey, and Justin; Haley and John; and Brandon and Margie, thanks for loving me even when I got it wrong as dad, step-dad, and father-in-law. There were simply too many times I should have been more caring than right. Words will not express how much I love you all, especially for giving us our precious grandkids.

Davis, Dabs, Kyler, Shealy Kate, Kylie, Sully, Olivia, and Porter, thanks to each of you for the joy you bring to Pops and CeCe with your overflowing love and abundant energy.

It's simply not possible to be blessed with two better parents than Mom and Pop Joe. Their unconditional love, support, and daily prayers have carried me my entire life.

Life would be a little boring if it were not for my siblings, Mike and Mitzi, who are always prepared to bring me down a notch or two. Laughing with you two is just as much fun now as when we were barefoot in the backyard on Jones Street. Thanks for your humor, love, and support. Joy and Tim, thanks for loving my siblings and always being supportive of our family "events."

Thanks to each and every team member of HORNE, both past and present. Each of you in some way has made us beBetter in our journey of building the Wise Firm. Thank you for *my* strong sense of belonging, a direct result of the trust and support you extended to me. You were patient with my mistakes and always provided me the benefit of good intentions.

To the secret prayer group that met weekly to pray for me and our firm, your prayers made a difference. Thank you for your love and commitment. You pulled the rope during good times and bad.

Lisa Taylor, you are simply an angel on earth.

Katie O'Brien, my executive assistant for my tenure as managing partner, you made me better as you served with me side by side every day. Thanks for your patience with me, for the many times you fell on the sword when I messed something up, and for always showing me how to serve humbly without complaint.

Kassi Rushing, thanks so much for your commitment and vision to help build the Wise Firm. Your creativity, communication skills, and wisdom helped propel us along our journey. You led early and often, and even when it was hard to lead, you did. You certainly helped me grow personally and as a leader. No one has contributed more than you to capturing and writing this story to share with others. This book would not be possible without your contributions. Your commitment, love, and faith to follow Jesus Christ are an inspiration to me.

Speaking of not possible, my weekly blog would simply not be without the care of Marla Gardner. Thanks so much for always making me beBetter with my blog and social media.

Thanks to Leslie Petro for always bringing that "I've got this" attitude and demonstrating to our team members and clients over and over that we appreciate them.

Special thanks to Wendy Eversole, Terry Traylor, and Karla Bennett, who served so unselfishly and kept the trains running on time despite my delays.

Roy Ward and Hugh Parker—how special is it to have two amazing mentors who gave freely of their wisdom, insights, love, and support? I am forever thankful to each of you, as this story and journey are simply not possible without your leadership. Roy, it was your vision that set our firm out to sail to explore the big sea. Hugh, it was your wisdom that grew me even when I didn't want to hear it.

I introduced several of our champions during the story of our journey. Thanks to each of them and our entire partner (ownership) group in May 2011, who embraced the Wise Firm vision; each said yes to beBetter. To the partner group, directors, and managers at HORNE today who lead us in taking the Wise Firm to the next level, thank you.

Thankfully, our list of champions who played significant roles or who came into their own as leaders during our journey and picked up the rope to make a big impact is rather lengthy. Naming everyone seems indulgent, although they all have made an impact on our journey. If we recognize those who were quick to pick up the rope and pull us forward on various initiatives, it includes Jason Saulters, Lee Klein, Anna Stroble, Jonathan Krebs, Scott Keller, Lacy Lyons, Mary Kathryn Allen, and Samir El Hage.

Special thanks to one of my best friends, business partner, and fishing buddy, Bruce Walt. Since we have been known to spend many hours on the water fishing for crappie (the best freshwater fish on the planet), we obviously had lots of conversations about how we could beBetter. You challenged me and listened more than anyone should have to tolerate.

No one achieves any significance without the help, love, and support of great friends. Thanks to some of my closest buds, Steve Napier, Alan Purdie, Kris Cole, and Bobby Reed. Joe Paul, my coach, friend, and advocate, early on in my career, you made such a positive impact on my leadership skills and taught me it starts by learning to lead yourself.

Everyone should be blessed with a personal board of directors as wise, supportive, and engaged as I have had over the last 30 years. It's obvious that I needed to hang around smart people, so thanks to each of you for answering my questions and sharing your knowledge, wisdom, and experience. Rick Dreher, Michelle Rivers, Dave Stende, Jeff Wald, Mark Koziel, Gail Perry, Andy and Matt Armamino, Gary Boomer, Rick Davis, Bill Hagaman, Jennifer Wilson, Alan Koltin, Larry Autrey, Alan Litwin, Lindsay Stevenson, Jim Wallace, David Erb, Chris Allgeretti, Kurt Gresens, Mary Elliott, Michelle Thompson, Jeff Kowieski, Carl Coburn, Bill Potvin, Darrell Strivens, Carl Shultz, and of course there are many others I apologize for not naming here.

Thanks to so many people I've had the joy and pleasure to encounter in my career. Every one of you made a difference in my life. Thanks for your kindness and helping me have a strong sense of belonging with your trust.

To the folks at Greenleaf Book Group, who turned a rough manuscript into a real story about building magnetic workplaces, thank you so much—especially Elizabeth, Lee, and Nathan, who overcame my lack of knowledge in writing and publishing. Speaking of writing, Jeff Wuorio, my ghostwriter, masterfully weaved my rambling and unconnected stories into a manuscript that had promise.

While I started these saying thanks for coincidences, it is no coincidence that I owe everything to my Lord and Savior, Jesus Christ. It is by Your abundant grace and unfailing love that I am even alive to enjoy this journey. Your peace is beyond description, and not only have You lifted me up from my mistakes, but You have blessed me more than I could ever deserve.

He currently serves on the board of The Mustard Seed, a Christian community for adults with developmental disabilities, and Empower Mississippi. He is a past board member of HORNE LLP, Friends of Children's Hospital, JDRF, Make-A-Wish Foundation, and AICPA Women's Initiative Executive Committee.

Joey earned a bachelor of business administration from the University of Mississippi. He attends St. Francis Catholic Church with his wife, Cathy.

About the Author

JOEY HAVENS, CPA, is currently serving HORNE as managing partner of strategic growth. He joined HORNE in 1984 and previously served as executive partner from 2012 to 2021, leading more than 1,800 team members to build the Wise Firm while passionately living out his life's calling to help others see and reach their full potential. Prior to being named executive partner in 2012, Joey served as HORNE's managing partner of health care services and the managing partner of government services, respectively.

Joey actively challenges the mainstays of business culture and strategic planning. He advocates growing leaders faster using holistic approaches and intentional sponsorship. In addition to his weekly *beBetter* blog, he is the author of numerous white papers and articles, including "Becoming the Firm of the Future," published by AICPA. He has coauthored four books during his career at HORNE.

Joey is an active member of CPA Practice Advisor's Top 30 Thought Leaders, where he works with other accounting professionals to help lead and shape the industry. Joey is a frequent presenter/teacher/facilitator on creating a culture of belonging, strategic planning, and leadership development and loves to teach young professionals the "ABCs to Outstanding."